RESOURCES FOR WRITING

FOR PUBLICATION

IN EDUCATION

SIDNEY B. KATZ
University of Pennsylvania

JEROME T. KAPES
Texas A&M University

PERRY A. ZIRKEL
Lehigh University

Teachers College Press
Teachers College, Columbia University
New York and London   1980

Copyright © 1980 by Sidney B. Katz, Jerome T. Kapes
and Perry A. Zirkel.
Published by Teachers College Press,
1234 Amsterdam Avenue, New York, New York 10027.

Library of Congress Cataloging in Publication Data

Katz, Sidney B.
  Resources for writing for publication in education.

  Bibliography: p.
  Includes index.
    1. Educational publishing—United States.
2. Copyright—United States.   I.   Kapes, Jerome T.,
joint author.   II.   Zirkel, Perry Alan, joint
author.   III.   Title.
Z286.E3K37   808'.066   79-27127
ISBN 0-8077-2579-X

Designed by Julie E. Scott
1 2 3 4 5 6 7 8 9   86 85 84 83 82 81 80
Manufactured in the United States of America

Table of Contents

TABLES

FIGURES

Acknowledgments

As with any book, no matter how small, many others besides the authors have played important roles. A large debt is owed to Marcia Berkow, Donna Yenolevich, and the other members of Lehigh University's School of Education secretarial staff for their diligence and persistence through numerous drafts. The assistance of research librarian Judith Mistichelli of the Lehigh University Linderman Library has been invaluable. Margot Eddy of the ERIC Clearinghouse on Higher Education and J. Robert Thornton of the Franklin Institute provided us with computer-assisted literature reviews. Professor Lewis Kurlantzick of the University of Connecticut School of Law was most generous in reviewing Chapter VII and making suggestions for changes. Mary L. Allison and Janet Clarke of Teachers College Press deserve a complimentary comment for putting up with three diverse personalities who worked on the completion of the manuscript from three different locations. Our supportive wives need also to be mentioned for their patience. Finally, we acknowledge our appreciation to Coffman Distinguished Professor Willam Van Til for graciously agreeing to write the book's foreword.

We thank all of them for their contributions.

S.B.K.
J.T.K.
P.A.Z.

Foreword

Sound practical help is steadily becoming available to educators who are or who hope to be published writers. This guide, *Resources for Writing for Publication in Education* by Sidney B. Katz, Jerome T. Kapes, and Perry A. Zirkel, brings together many such aids.

The guide is evidence of a growing recognition that educators need concrete down-to-earth assistance in their publication efforts. In the early 1950s when I created the course Writing for Educational Publications at George Peabody College for Teachers, it was, so far as I have been able to determine, the first of its kind in the nation. But during the decade 1968 through 1977, a period when I regularly offered Writing for Educational Publications at Indiana State University, the number of courses, workshops, clinics, and programs for writers of educational publications continually increased. For instance, the American Association of Colleges for Teacher Education and the Association for Supervision and Curriculum Development included sessions on writing for professional publications in their annual convention programs. The Association of Teacher Educators went a step further and sponsored national and regional workshops of several days duration on writing for educational publications. Some perceptive college administrators replaced exhortations to faculty members (which often accompanied explanations of why salary increments and promotions were being denied) with tangible weekend workshops for potential and published writers for educational publications.

The Katz, Kapes, and Zirkel guide is a useful tool both for participants in such courses, clinics, and workshops and for individual educators and psychologists alone in their offices who are attempting to find their way through the maze of getting published. The authors have provided a genuine professional service in bringing together and commenting thoughtfully on the wide variety of resources now available for educators and psychologists who write and researchers who want to share their findings. I have used preliminary drafts of this guide in the workshops and clinics I currently conduct in universities, and they have invariably proven helpful.

You will find this guide useful whether you have published widely or are contemplating publication. Even the most experienced educational writer or psychologist is not familiar with all the resources the authors have brought together. Whether you are finding your own way or participating in an organized program concerning educational writing, this impressive assemblage of material will be of value to you.

WILLIAM VAN TIL
Coffman Distinguished Professor
Emeritus of Education
Indiana State University

Introduction

For the beginning or infrequent author, a lack of familiarity with the tools of the trade—writing and research materials, vehicles for professional and creative production, regulations concerning publication—may inhibit the research, writing, and publication necessary for professional advancement and growth. Given the demands on professional educators for publication productivity, the competition for limited publishing opportunities, and the need for quality in educational communication, some form of aid to the novice seems appropriate and necessary. This book is intended to reduce some of the unfamiliarity by surveying the literature and resources available to graduate students and faculty members interested in writing for publication in education. This work is not a research guide; the authors assume that the reader is at least acquainted with, if not fully conversant in, research design and methodology. Rather, the purpose of this book is to familiarize prospective authors with the references and resources that will clarify, simplify, and help organize their knowledge and skills so they can increase the likelihood of being published.

This book is organized to focus on the three related, but discrete, forms of professional communication: the conference, the journal, and the book. However, the information presented and discussed in all seven chapters has potential benefits above and beyond publication and the tenure and monetary rewards that could accrue. Clear, useful, and productive professional communication and interaction are the objectives. Conferences, journals, and books are vehicles for realizing these goals.

The first chapter stresses the "Importance of Publication" from the educator's personal point of view—professional advancement, tenure, prestige. The "Conference and Convention Papers," "Journals," and "Books and Monographs" chapters discuss how to approach each of these areas of communication. Chapter V, "Indices," surveys the information sources and library research tools necessary for the generation and development of ideas and creative educational thought. The sixth chapter looks at the other side of the research task, putting it all on paper in a coherent and publishable form. The last chapter discusses copyright as it pertains to the author and consumer.

In any event, this book is not a step-by-step how-to guide. Rather, it attempts to organize in a readily usable form the many and varied tools generally available to, but not fully known by, the educator qua writer. The authors' assumption is that you have to be aware of what is out there before you can best select and use it to your own advantage. Experience has shown that even senior faculty are not as conversant with the tools of the trade as might be assumed.

This book began, in fact, as a project intended for in-house use by faculty members and doctoral students of the Lehigh University School of Education where all three authors met for the first time during the 1977–78 school year. As such things do, the little manual kept growing until the authors decided to share the information on a wider basis.

As should be the case in a field so broad and varied as education, the three authors represent diverse backgrounds, roles, and interests. Sidney B. Katz, now a doctoral student at the University of Pennsylvania, is a school psychologist and special educator. Jerome T. Kapes, presently an associate professor of vocational education at Texas A&M University, has proven credentials in vocational and career education, educational research, and vocational guidance. Perry A. Zirkel, dean and professor of the School of Education at Lehigh University, has focused his research, writing, and teaching in bilingual-multicultural education, educational administration, and school law. Although this book is an initial publication effort for the lead author, both of the latter authors have numerous publications to their credit.

1
IMPORTANCE
OF PUBLICATION

The importance of publication in education can be viewed from a number of perspectives. The most obvious and important perspective for those individuals engaged in the struggle of moving up the professional career ladder concerns the rewards that result from publishing and the punishments for not publishing. For this group of individuals, the question of the importance of publishing can be answered directly by assessing the extent to which the threat of "publish or perish" is real. Over the years, a number of books and articles have addressed this issue. For those interested in a descriptive look at the academic reward structure as it was 40 or 20 years ago, *The Academic Man: A Study in the Sociology of a Profession* (Wilson, 1942) and *The Academic Marketplace* (Caplow & McGee, 1958) are classic works for their time. However important publication was in days gone by, there is every reason to believe it plays an even larger role today.

MONETARY REWARDS FOR PUBLICATION

Katz (1973) in a recent study of faculty salaries, promotions, and productivity at a large public university reported that most chairmen and department heads felt that research ability, publication record, and national reputation were the factors considered most important in deciding salary and promotion at their institutions. Using a linear regression model, Katz found that an ordinary article adds $18 and an excellent article $102 to a faculty member's yearly salary. A book, in contrast, was worth $230 a year in additional salary. In a similar study, Seigfried and White (1973) examined the salaries of the economics faculty at the University of Wisconsin in relationship to various publishing and nonpublishing activities. While other factors besides publication (e.g., experience and administrative duties) were found to be significantly related to salary, an article was worth between $344 and $395 depending on the journal, while other publications were worth only $76. Monographs were not found to influence salary significantly.

In what will probably become a classic study of the academic reward structure, Tuckman (1976), with the aid of the American Council on Education, analyzed data from a national cross-sectional sample of 53,034 faculty members from 301 institutions of all types. The data were examined separately for males and females using a large linear regression model with salary as the dependent variable and numerous independent variables, which included articles and books written, teaching excellence, public service, administrative experience, and geographical and professional field variables. The outcome of this analysis revealed that salary increased significantly with each article published, with one to two articles worth $714 more annually for males and $181 more for females. Although females received less than males for their first two articles, they increased their salary at a greater rate than males as their article productivity increased. In all cases except the one to two and 50-plus article categories, females earned more than males for each published article. In the case of book publications, however, a small amount of salary increase was found for males and none for females. In fact, in the 10-plus book category there is an actual decline in salary, which Tuckman speculates is due to the amount of time spent on writing, resulting in a neglect of other activities also important in the reward structure. Considering all the independent variables in Tuckman's analysis, article publication is the only area in which females gain greater rewards than males for the same productivity.

In addition to looking at the entire academic system, Tuckman conducted separate analysis within various fields. Education was grouped with law, medicine, and pharmacy for this analysis. In education, one to two articles were worth $877, while law faculty members received $2,290 more for the same number of articles. An education faculty member with over 50 articles earned $4,565 more than nonpublishers; while the law faculty member received $5,407 additional salary. Faculty members in medicine and pharmacy did not experience any increase in salary in relationship to articles published although, on the average, they published many more articles than did law or education faculty. In the case of book publication, Tuckman found that only in education was an effect on salary evident. In education, a faculty member with ten or more books earned $1,311 more yearly salary than a faculty member with no books. The most sobering of Tuckman's findings is the fact that "the teaching variable is not statistically significant in any of the regressions. This is a somewhat surprising finding for the field of education since one might hope that at least in this field a good teaching job would be recognized" (p. 75). Both public service and administrative experience had some positive effect on salary in the education field.

When Tuckman examined the direct lifetime returns of publication, he found that the earlier in a person's career a publication occurs, the larger the lifetime salary returns. According to him, "for females as well as males, the assistant professor stands to gain the most from publication" (p. 86). This advantage occurs because a salary increment once gained tends to continue as an additional part of a person's salary throughout a professional lifetime. As a way to estimate the indirect lifetime return of publishing, Tuckman used promotion instead of salary as the dependent variable in a regression analysis, which simultaneously controlled for the effects of other probable influences on promotion (e.g., teaching, public service, experience). For promotion to associate professor, a male with one article had a 4.1 percent chance of promotion while a similar female had a 10.2 percent chance. With 25 articles, male probabilities were 31.1 percent and female probabilities 21.1 percent. The effect that articles had on promotion to full professor was much smaller at all levels of article production, but consistently favored females. Further information on the complete analysis of the effects of publication in education can be found in Tuckman and Hagmann (1976) "An Analysis of the Reward Structure in Two Disciplines."

In a study similar to Tuckman's, but based on an extensive survey of 453 department heads from 134 universities of three types (i.e., research universities, doctoral-granting universities, and comprehensive universities and colleges), Centra (1977) investigated the methods and criteria used to evaluate faculty for tenure, salary, and promotions. According to responses obtained concerning scholarship and research, Centra found that "in general, the number of articles published in quality journals, the number of books of which a faculty member is the sole or senior author, and the quality of one's research and publications as judged by peers at the institution are the three most important types of information used" (p. 12). However, there were striking differences among the three types of institutions studied. Research universities tend to put more emphasis on articles in quality journals and peer judgement of research quality and least emphasis on unpublished papers and self, department head, or dean evaluations. Comprehensive universities and colleges place less emphasis on most of the scholarship and research criteria examined in the study, with doctoral-granting universities falling in between.

Using discriminate function analysis with the 16 scholarship and research criteria examined in the study, Centra found two dimensions or factors. The first contrasts "books, monographs, and papers" on one extreme with "grants received" on the other extreme. The second dimension contrasts "evaluation by deans and self" with "peer evaluations of articles in quality journals and professional awards." Education, which was grouped with other professional fields, was located in discriminate space towards the "grants" end of dimension one and the "peer evaluation, articles and awards" end of dimension two when research universities were considered. However, for doctoral-granting and comprehensive universities and colleges, the professions were grouped closest to the "evaluation by dean and self" end of dimension two. Considering all three areas typically used to evaluate faculty (teaching, research, and service), service was of least importance in all three types of institutions, with scholarship and research most important at research universities and teaching most important at the other two types of institutions.

Separate studies by Hall and Blackburn (1975) and Ladd and Lipset (1976) provide empirical insights into the allied question of the relationship between teaching and research. Lewis (1967) provides the perspective of earlier empirical studies showing that the relationship between promotions and publications may have been largely mythical in the first half of the twentieth century.

CONTRIBUTIONS AND USEFULNESS OF PUBLICATION

A second perspective from which the importance of publication in education can be viewed concerns the contributions and usefulness to the field of the material currently being published. In this light, Showalter (1978) discussed the effect that the tight job market is having on publication productivity in the liberal arts colleges. He pointed out that historically liberal arts college faculty have been made up of "locals," who are primarily loyal to their college campus and engage in teaching and service as opposed to research, and "cosmopolitans," who are oriented towards the national or international research community and who will soon leave for greener academic pastures. Since the more restricted job market may not provide a place for cosmopolitans to go, Showalter suggests "putting new emphasis on publication, increasing institutional rewards for the writer of papers, articles, and monographs" (p. 170). He takes this point of view because, in the

absence of faculty mobility, entire liberal arts faculties could even-
tually be made up of locals who do not engage in research and
publication, thus resulting in academic stagnation for the institution as a whole.

Murray (1975), writing in the *Journal of Legal Education,* takes
a divergent point of view from that presented by Showalter. According to Murray, most of what is written and published in law
journals is done by members of the teaching legal profession and
is done under pressure of a publish or perish nature. As he pointed
out, "the consequence of this pressure is that the law professor
finds himself pursuing a life style which naturally diminishes his
daily teaching preparation and leaves little time for student contact of any real value" (p. 568). Furthermore, Murray doubts the
quality and usefulness of much of what is published under this
current system. Therefore, he recommends less publishing by law
teaching faculties, which would result in the dual benefit of better
but fewer articles (which will result in a better chance of an article
being read) and more time for teaching (which will result in
better law school graduates). Meyer (1972) echoes Murray's mes-
sage for university faculty members in general, concluding that,
"We can no longer afford a system that forces grown-up professors
to play games" (p. 104).

The question of how to evaluate faculty publication is discussed
by Kingsley (1976). She reviewed various methods from simple
numerical counting to complex rating and weighting schemes. Included among these schemes are the Van Til (1973) method
(assigning a grade of A, B, or C based on the extent to which the
author makes it through the various publishing hurdles), and the
citation method (see e.g., Narin & Garside, 1972) based on the
number of times an author is cited in other sources. Various citation indices are available to help in this latter method (see Chapter V). Pitts and Fletcher's study (1978) presents a view of how
publications are prioritized for faculty promotion decisions among
southeastern colleges and universities. Articles in national refereed
journals received the top rating by administrators.

Just as authors are evaluated by the (publishing) company they
keep, so too are institutions evaluated by the number and quality

of articles produced by their faculties. Cox and Catt (1977) examined APA journals to determine the productivity ratings of graduate programs in psychology. West (1978) conducted a similar study within education counting the number of articles published in both the *Review of Educational Research* and the *American Educational Research Journal* between 1970 and 1976. From his analysis, he concluded that the institutions highly ranked in terms of prestige [as measured by Walberg (1972) in a previous study] do not dominate the pages of AERA journals.

ACTIVITIES PROMOTING PUBLICATION

Perhaps a third perspective from which the importance of publication in education can be seen is in the number of books, articles, and other activities within education that deal with this topic. The fact that this text is being read is testimony to the importance placed on publication by those who have purchased it. Several other excellent books have also appeared that deal with the topic of publishing in one form or another in education-related fields. Among these books are: Mullins (1977) *A Guide to Writing and Publishing in the Social and Behavioral Sciences,* van Leunen (1978a) *A Handbook for Scholars,* and Appelbaum and Evans (1978) *How to Get Happily Published.* Furthermore, articles appearing in widely read education journals, such as Van Til's (1978) column "Editorial Roulette" in *Phi Delta Kappan* and Kaplan's (1977) column "Survival Talk for Educators—Tenure and Promotion" in the *Journal of Teacher Education,* attest to the urgency of the topic. There is also a journal devoted exclusively to publishing in academia—*Scholarly Publishing: A Journal for Authors and Publishers* (1978).

Focus on the topic of academic publishing is evident in other forms too. Van Til (no date) has produced a video tape, *Writing for Educational Publication,* which is available from the Closed Circuit Television Center at the Indiana State University, and has conducted numerous workshops around the country on that theme. The American Association of Colleges of Teacher Education (AACTE) and Education Press of America jointly sponsored a program on Publishing in Education at the 1978 annual meeting of AACTE. The Association for Supervision and Curriculum Development, the International Consortium for Options in Public Education, the International Reading Association, and the American Association of School Administrators have included such sessions in their recent annual conferences. The Association of Teacher Educators sponsored a centrally located miniclinic on writing for publication in the spring of 1978, and Phi Delta Kappa offered four regional workshops on this topic during the fall of 1978.

Lastly, several universities have started to offer courses on publishing in hopes of improving their students' and faculties' achievements in this area. Van Til has been offering just such a course at Indiana State University since 1967, Professor Vincent Rogers initiated such a course in 1978 at the University of Connecticut, and Zirkel (a coauthor of this text) has recently developed a minicourse on this subject at Lehigh University.

In summary, both the need and the resources for quality publication in education appear to be great. All that is lacking is the motivation to act. As Van Til (1973) has pointed out, "the art of writing is the art of applying the seat of the pants to the seat of the chair . . . writing is one-tenth inspiration and nine-tenths perspiration" (p. 701).

2
CONFERENCE AND
CONVENTION PAPERS

The vast numbers of associations and special interest groups that hold conferences and conventions each year suggest that all interested educators should be able to find a forum for presenting ideas and findings in their areas of interest. Records of conference proceedings reveal that many papers are presented by graduate students or other previously unpublished authors. For presentation at a conference, a report need not be in manuscript perfect form. At the submission stage, an abstract of the paper will frequently suffice, although technical and methodological requirements for a proposed conference paper are more stringent. Since one factor in selecting a manuscript for publication in a journal is previous research production (Frantz, 1968), presentation of a paper at a conference can provide the professional credibility useful for journal consideration. Also, interaction with others with similar research interests can be beneficial in honing professional skills.

9

Informal feedback from colleagues may be more informative than the comments of an overworked editor and, in practical terms, presenting a paper usually means travel and expense money from one's school or agency. All these factors make presentation of a paper at a conference an appropriate starting point for professional publication. Surprisingly, however, there are few how-tos specifically concerning conference papers in the literature.

SELECTING THE FORUM

Selecting a conference for submitting a manuscript or abstract is not as simple as finding names, dates, and contact persons. Most conferences have specific submission procedures. Convention themes must be recognized, schedules adhered to, rules for presentation followed, and, when the contributor is not a member of the convening organization, often member sponsors need to be obtained.

Sponsoring Associations

For information regarding conferences of educational associations, three sources are available: *Educator's World: The Standard Guide to American-Canadian Educational Associations, Conventions, Foundations, Publications, and Research Centers* (1972), the *NEA Handbook* (1973), and Fisk's *Encyclopedia of Associations* (1978). *Educator's World* covers local, state, provincial, and national associations, conventions, and so forth. The *NEA Handbook* offers information on national, regional, and state teachers associations, their publications, and convention dates. The *Encyclopedia of Associations* is an annual, which comes in three volumes and includes a separate listing for education associations. Each entry contains information about the association including address, phone numbers, membership interests, divisions, journals published, and dates for association meetings.

Meetings of individual organizations (e.g., American Association of School Administrators, Council for Exceptional Children, American Educational Research Association, American Vocational

Association) are typically announced far in advance in their official journals and newsletters.

Calendars of Meetings

Since one's own organization(s) may not be the preferred vehicle for presenting particular ideas and research, access to information about other associations and meetings is necessary for finding the best forum. *The Chronicle of Higher Education* publishes a "Calendar" each spring, which lists locations, dates of events, and conference contact persons for over 200 organizations and their respective regional and divisional meetings. Each month the *American Psychologist* contains a listing of upcoming national and international conferences in psychology and related fields. The *APA Monitor, Chronicle of Higher Education, Educational Researcher,* and other organization publications frequently contain advertisements and announcements for meetings and conventions.

The Communication Support Division of the U.S. Office of Education's Office of Public Affairs publishes twice a year a comprehensive list of educational organizations' meetings. Every June and December this list provides addresses, telephone numbers, meeting dates, locations, and, when available, themes for the organizations and their subgroups holding meetings during the forthcoming six months.

Calls for Papers

Typically, professional associations will announce their meeting(s) and request papers and symposia via a call for papers, which is distributed to members far enough in advance of the conference so that papers and topics may be prepared. This call will list the rules and guidelines for participation, topics requested, contact persons, and other pertinent information. Some organizations publish calls for papers in their periodicals as does the American Educational Research Association's (AERA) announcement (Appendix A) in *Educational Researcher* (1978). A shorter call for papers by the International Reading Association

FIGURE 1: Example of a Short Call for Papers

CALL FOR RESEARCH PAPERS AND SYMPOSIA

TWENTY-FOURTH ANNUAL CONVENTION • APRIL 23-27, 1979 • ATLANTA, GEORGIA

INTERNATIONAL READING ASSOCIATION

To provide opportunities for dissemination, discussion and critique of research, the Studies and Research Committee announces this call for papers. There are two categories for reporting research: 1) single paper proposals and 2) symposium proposals. The Studies and Research Committee reviews only research papers in which evidence is presented regarding ideas, hypotheses or programs. Reports of innovative programs, teacher preparation services and other topics that do not include research are reviewed by the Program Committee, and appropriate application forms (available from International Reading Association, 800 Barksdale Road, P.O. Box 8139, Newark, Delaware 19711, U.S.A.) should be used. Students, professors, and other professionals from reading and related fields are encouraged to submit papers and symposia.

should be titled and should not contain the name(s) of the author(s) and affiliation(s). Proposals must be submitted with an official Research Cover Sheet.

Symposium Proposal Requirements. A 150-word abstractions and their interrelationships are required. All material should be double-spaced and typewritten. Examples of abstracts may be found in journals published by the American Psychological Association. Abstracts and previews should be titled and should not contain the names of the contributors and their affiliations. Proposals must be submitted with an official Research Cover Sheet.

Number of Copies. Five copies of the abstract and the paper or the symposium preview are necessary. Photocopies or mimeographed copies are acceptable. Postcard and Stamps. One self-addressed and stamp-

Deadline. September 1

Types of Proposals. Single paper: report of completed research. About 20-25 minutes will be allotted for each paper accepted. Symposium: a group presentation of research on a specific theme or problem. A total of 2¾ hours will be allocated for each symposium which may be used at the discretion of the organizers.

Single Paper Proposal Requirements. A 150-word abstract and a 1000-word paper are required. Both should be double-spaced and typewritten. Examples of abstracts may be found in journals published by the American Psychological Association. Abstracts and papers

ed postcard is needed to communicate receipt of the proposal.

Criteria for Proposals. Proposals will be judged in terms of the significance of the topic, the quality of the theoretical/conceptual rationale, the adequacy of the methods for collecting evidence, the analysis of the evidence and the interpretations and/or conclusions. Incomplete proposals will be returned.

Where to Obtain Research Cover Sheet. Research Department, International Reading Association, 800 Barksdale Road, P.O. Box 8139, Newark, Delaware 19711, U.S.A.

From *Educational Researcher*, 1978, 7(3), 2. Copyright 1978 by the American Educational Research Association. Reprinted by permission.

(IRA), published in *Educational Researcher* (1978), typifies the call published with the intent of soliciting papers from members of related organizations (Figure 1). Other organizations place brief advertisements and announcements in periodicals indicating how interested parties may obtain further information on a given conference (Figure 2). This last method is often used by organizations that wish to receive paper proposals from a wider audience than their own memberships, by conferences not affiliated with any single organization or without a membership, and by institutions holding one-shot conferences. Some groups limit conference participation to invited presenters on designated issues. Membership in such closed groups is based upon proven expertise in a given field, so a record of presentations and publications is an important vehicle to these prestige groups.

In the AERA's call for papers (Appendix A) note the detailed

FIGURE 2:   Example of a Brief Call for Papers from an Outside Organization

The Association of American Medical Colleges will hold its 17th Annual Conference on Research in Medical Education (RIME) in conjunction with its 89th Annual Meeting, October 22–26, 1978, at the New Orleans Hilton Hotel, New Orleans, Louisiana. The conference is a forum for the presentation and discussion of scientific papers concerned with the process of medical education as well as a forum for the presentation of topic-orientated symposia. Papers will be considered for formal presentation as well as presentation in Poster Sessions. Papers and proposals for symposia must be postmarked by May 30, 1978. Guidelines for the preparation of papers and symposia may be obtained by writing to: RIME Conference/AAMC, 1 Dupont Circle, N.W., Suite 200, Washington, D.C. 20036.

requirements for paper submission and presentation. The entire call, in fact, covers eight pages. IRA's call (Figure 1) is less detailed but provides sufficient guidelines for topic selection and manuscript preparation. Figure 2 is a very brief announcement by the Association of American Medical Colleges indicating dates, location, theme, and procedure for obtaining more complete information and guidelines.

PRESENTING THE PAPER

There are few articles in the educational literature about preparing and presenting papers for conferences. The instructions for preparing a journal article (see Chapter III, Preparing the Article) are equally applicable to conference papers and adequately supplement the mechanical guidelines in calls for papers. Research, methodology, and sophistication of language in the conference paper are similar to that of the well-prepared article. The information on indices in Chapter V and style manuals and writing guides in Chapter VI are also relevant for preparing conference papers.

Yorkey (1978), writing in the newsletter for Teachers of English to Speakers of Other Languages (TESOL), presents a very useful set of suggestions in "How to Prepare and Present a Professional Paper." Among the many suggestions offered, he recommends rehearsing the paper as in a professional performance, checking the meeting room and equipment ahead of time, opening a presentation with some spontaneous remarks, and repeating questions that come from the audience. For the individual who is presenting a paper for the first time, a complete reading of Yorkey's article is recommended. In fact, even veteran presenters may find his comprehensive list of suggestions worth going over as a means of self-improvement.

In a work directed to managers and other professionals, Mambert (1976) presents a program aimed at developing oral communication skills. He offers a ten-unit, self-paced course with stated learning objectives, exercises to follow, and tests for assessment of oral communication skills. This program would appear to be useful for persons uncertain about presenting a paper at a conference or for those who do not feel their speaking and communication abilities are adequate.

Schlosberg (1965) offers hints on presenting a paper at a conference. His primary emphasis is on how to speak before an audience and present information verbally. In a satirical article, Zurcher (1977) wryly comments on the various poses and roles presenters seem to assume at meetings. Although the main point of this article is clearly academic humor, the author vividly describes the various shortcomings that convention speakers often exhibit.

PUBLISHING A PAPER IN ERIC

An intermediate step between conferences and journals, which provides an opportunity to publish a conference paper or other work, is the Educational Research Information Center (ERIC) system through its subject area clearinghouses. ERIC frequently requests copies of papers presented at conferences. An author may also submit articles, manuscripts, monographs, and so on directly to an appropriate clearinghouse without ERIC solicitation. Note in Appendix A that AERA encourages participants to submit copies of papers to a relevant ERIC clearinghouse. A work, if accepted, is stored in hard copy at the clearinghouse, reprinted on microfiche, and housed in various ERIC resource centers around the country. Works accepted are also abstracted and indexed in *Resources in Education,* where a list of clearinghouses and addresses may be found. A complete list of all ERIC clearinghouses and services, along with their addresses, is provided in Appendix B.

ERIC reserves the right to reproduce manuscripts it houses upon request by interested users via the ERIC Document Reproduction Service (EDRS). Copyright for these works remains with the author or original publisher, and the author's permission to reproduce copies is required for all users except ERIC.

Documents must be submitted in duplicate to either a specific clearinghouse or, preferably, to the ERIC Processing and Reference Facility (EPRF) Acquisitions Department (see Appendix B).

For more detailed information on the process of submission to and selection by ERIC, refer to *Submitting Documents to ERIC,* available from EPRF, or to *How to Use ERIC,* available from the National Institute of Education, Washington, D.C. 20208. The ERIC system also aids the writer and researcher via its computerized search services.

3
JOURNALS

Journals seem to be the medium of professional communication that best fits the phrase "all things to all people" (excepting money. It is the rare professional journal that makes payment to authors. The wider market periodicals, such as *Learning* and *Psychology Today,* are the ones that can pay for articles). The sheer number and range of journals available make it possible for every prospective author to find some channel that is appropriate for reporting his or her ideas and research. For example, the *Current Index to Journals in Education* lists over 700 education and education-related journals. *Education Index* lists nearly 250. Announcements of new periodicals are frequent. The significant issues for authors are finding the appropriate journal and writing with an understanding of what shapes the acceptance-rejection decisions of journal editors. For each of these issues there are resources to which the potential author may refer.

FINDING A JOURNAL

Comprehensive Journal Directories

Although finding the most appropriate journal for a particular article may require a broad knowledge of current journals, there are compendia of journal descriptions available that help simplify the selection process. The most extensive is the annually revised *Ulrich's International Periodicals Directory* (UIPD). It lists over 60,000 periodicals throughout the world, grouped by subject headings, arranged alphabetically within subjects, and cross-indexed by subject area. Although UIPD includes journals in all disciplines, the education section contains over 2,000 titles from the United States and foreign countries. Information provided includes country of origin, publisher's name and address, editor, circulation, special features (e.g., advertising, book reviews), format, and indices in which the journal is listed. This last category, important for reference librarians in particular, is both a strength and a weakness of UIPD. Palais (1974) compared index references for a number of periodicals in UIPD and reports that many references are missing for a sample of major periodicals.

UIPD is supplemented by *Ulrich's Irregular Serials and Annuals,* which, like UIPD, is revised yearly. This compendium provides data similar to that in UIPD for over 30,000 "serials, annuals, continuations, conference proceedings, and other publications issued irregularly or less frequently than two times a year" (UIPD, p. xii). A clear advantage of these two volumes is their frequent updating and revision. This is particularly important when obtaining information on journals with regular turnovers of editorial staff and resulting new addresses for submission.

A less comprehensive, but more detailed, resource is Marquis Academic Media's *Directory of Publishing Opportunities* (DPO) (1975). Over 2,600 entries, 198 under education, represent 69 specific fields of interest. DPO includes "only those periodicals . . . that represent real publishing opportunities and accept submissions in English" (p. ix). The data provided on journals includes most of that in UIPD along with subscription rates, frequency of publication, a statement of editorial purpose, average number of articles per issue, the intended audience, style requirements, average article length, number of copies to be submitted, payment (if any) to author, number of reprints to author, holder of copyright and manuscript rights, and whether criticism of the manuscript is provided. As of this writing, an updated edition of the DPO has not been released, and because of rapid changes in journals, some information contained in the 1975 edition may not be up to date.

Although it contains information on all types of journals, *The Standard Periodical Directory 1979–80* (1978) lists over 2,000 journals specifically under education. This figure does *not* include related journals listed under children, school administration, and so forth. The volume provides a frequently updated alphabetical listing of journals by title, journal publisher, editor, editor address and telephone number, a brief editorial statement of content, subscription cost, circulation, and format.

Another very useful directory, because it includes an abstract for each entry, is *Magazines for Libraries* (Katz & Richards, 1978). It contains over 4,500 titles covering 96 specific areas. In the area of education, over 150 periodicals are reviewed with information on title, date founded, frequency of publication, price, editor, publisher and address, circulation, audience, and a number of other useful data. This information is followed by an abstract of approximately 50 to 250 words.

If an author is seeking to reach a specific geographical area, the yearly updated *Ayer Directory of Publications* is a helpful guide. It lists journals by state, country, province, and other geographical entities for periodicals published in the United States, Puerto Rico, the Virgin Islands, Canada, the Bahamas, Bermuda, Panama, and the Philippines.

Other sources that could help the prospective journal author find a publishing outlet include several of the major sections in the *1978 Writer's Market* (Koester & Hillman, 1977) and the "Writer's Market" part of *The Writer's Handbook* (1978). Both these sources are reviewed more extensively in Chapter IV.

Education Journal Directories

There are a number of publications pertaining exclusively to education. The most extensive is *America's Education Press* (Educational Press Association of America, 1976). Over 1,400 journals from the United States and Canada are indexed in the 33rd edition. This figure includes major journals, state and provincial education association newsletters and journals, children's magazines, and other publications of members of the Educational Press Association of America. Excluded are publications with circulations of less than 200 and those journals whose editors failed to respond to requests for information. The periodicals are grouped under three main categories and many specific subareas (e.g., educational theory, social studies, etc.). Information provided is similar to that in DPO. A major advantage of *America's Education Press* is its low cost, making it readily available for individual ownership. It is revised approximately every two years. The 34th edition, however, will be somewhat more costly and will include only the periodicals of association members, decreasing the range of contents markedly (Gillespie, 1979).

Camp and Schwark's *Guide to Periodicals in Education and Its Academic Disciplines* (1975) reviews 602 education and education-related journals published in the United States. This volume replaces Camp's *Guide to Periodicals in Education* (1968). Camp and Schwark's *Guide* provides subscription data, editorial contact information, a statement of editorial policy, advice on manuscript preparation, time required for manuscript disposition, and copyright holder information. The information on time required for a manuscript acceptance-rejection decision is a particularly useful feature of this guide. However, not all journal entries contain complete information, which is apparently the result of journal editors failing to provide it.

Education/Psychology Journals: A Scholars' Guide (Arnold & Doyle, 1975) contains descriptions of 122 journals selected for their appropriateness to education and psychology students and scholars. It provides information about the editor, publisher, subscription rates, article content, special features, acceptance-rejection procedures, manuscript disposition, style, payment, and reprints. One item of interest among the various pieces of information provided reveals the fact that a number of major journals require page payment from authors or payment for inclusion of tables, figures, and the like. A problem with Arnold and Doyle's selection procedure is the exclusion of some of the major journals; for example, the *Journal of School Psychology,* the major publication for that field, is not reviewed.

An outdated and out-of-print publication, the *Scholars Guide to Journals of Education and Educational Psychology* (Lins & Rees, 1965) , is useful in one special respect. Schoenfeld's introduction to the volume constitutes a primer for the prospective author. It provides a good description of the process an author follows in preparing and submitting an article for publication, advice to the author about the stages of manuscript preparation and selection, a philosophy of journal communication, and the concerns an author should be aware of in preparing a manuscript for publication. The volume itself includes information on 135 journals, but the information was collected in 1964.

Another comprehensive source is *Education and Education-Related Serials: A Directory* (Krepal & Duvall, 1977) . In addition to the usual basic information, the entries include samples of recent article titles.

The *Publication Manual of the American Psychological Association* (American Psychological Association, 1974) provides a list of APA journals, descriptions of these journals, their editorial practices, and references to where and when recent editorial statements have been made. Although a number of non-APA journals use this manual for style format, the descriptive, editorial, and other information is limited to APA journals.

A volume that addresses primarily, but not exclusively, Canadian publications is Cameron and Goding's *A Guide to Publishing in Education* (1977) . In addition to publication frequency, style, decision time, content areas, index locations, and so forth, many editors of the journals included have provided personal comments pertaining to editorial policy and unappreciated author behavior [e.g., a major gripe of one editor was that articles were "submitted by people who obviously have never seen a copy of the magazine and know nothing of its nature" (p. 14)].

Specific lists of journals in reading (Bowden, Hutchison, & Mountain, 1977), language arts (Bowden & Mountain, 1975), and ESL teachers (Haskell, 1978) are available for persons seeking to publish in these areas. Annotated lists are provided for, respectively, 28 reading journals, 29 language arts journals, and 80 journals, newsletters, and publications for ESL teachers in the United States and Canada. They include editors' names and addresses, publication frequencies, manuscript requirements, and format.

Although journal directories can simplify selection of a journal, it is still necessary to refer to the chosen journal for specific information. Few of the directories include, for example, two critical limiting factors—whether the journal takes a thematic approach and whether or not their articles are refereed. Nor do the directories attempt to evaluate the journals. Studies are available (e.g., Koulack & Kesselman, 1975; Luce & Johnson, 1978) that provide ratings of professional journals by educators and psychologists. Editor changes, announcements of changes in manuscript requirements and policies, and the stylistic "look and feel" of journals cannot be included in the various compendia. Also, because of the large number of new or relatively obscure journals in print, many will not be found in any of the resources listed. To help readers find some of these new journals, a list of titles, editors, and addresses of some new journals is provided in Appendix C.

PREPARING THE ARTICLE

Writing an article to improve the likelihood of acceptance by a journal involves an understanding of what good writing is in general as well as what makes for a good quality professional paper. Resources for improving an author's quality of writing are reviewed later (see Chapter VI, Style Manuals and Writing Guides). Writing for journals is a special subset of authorship, and a number of experts in this area have offered advice on what it takes to be a good writer for journals. Many are frequent authors, others editors. All reflect long-term or detailed experience in the art of publishing in journals and what good journal writing is all about.

Van Til (1973), in a *Phi Delta Kappan* article titled "Writing for Publication," provides a thoughtful discussion and many suggestions to the aspiring educational writer. His suggestions include:

- submit book reviews as a way of getting started
- write articles based on teaching experiences
- write articles based on one's doctoral dissertation—undertaken immediately after completion and written in a popularized form
- take the initiative—don't wait to be invited to write an article
- block out a chunk of time for writing—develop discipline in sticking to a writing schedule
- query editors persistently about what they want and what is happening with a submitted manuscript.

Miller (1974), chairman of the publication committee of the Association for Supervision and Development, offers six suggestions for improving the chances for an article's acceptance. He addresses his comments to:

- analyzing reasons for writing
- being prepared for the work involved in writing an article
- planning the approach to matching article, intended audience, and journal
- giving attention to writing style, technique, and the mechanics of manuscript preparation
- getting critical reaction to the manuscript
- selecting the type of article content and focus with care.

Miller's overall emphasis is on recognizing purpose, focus, and audience, and how these relate to journals. As a way to get started in writing for journals, he echos Van Til's recommendation to submit book reviews to journals.

Etzold (1976) discusses the means by which an author can implement suggestions like Miller's. He speaks of organizational schemes [e.g., "Essays with three sections, topics with three aspects . . . all seem somehow to balance more mutually and convincingly than two or four." (p. 614)], early introduction of topic information in the paper, proper paragraph transition, the importance of grammatical writing, and the need for critical feedback from others. Etzold also emphasizes the importance of recognizing the intended audience for the article, finding the appropriate journal (s), and writing to fit the journal to which it will be submitted. One factor Etzold does not address is the impropriety of submitting an article to more than one journal at a time because of the amount of time, energy, and money expended in reviewing a manuscript submitted to a journal (or book) publisher.

Rainey (1973) summarizes 19 personal and work characteristics 200 authors reported as important for a person writing with the intent to publish. These authors emphasized the following:

- a questioning mind
- knowledge of a discipline
- insatiable reading habits
- language facility
- a story to tell
- timeliness
- research mindedness
- a reflective mind
- self-discipline and self-criticism
- dissatisfaction (with the discipline as it exists)
- knowledge of needs (of the publication)
- creative loneliness and regularity of writing
- desire for recognition
- desire to improve educational practices
- flair for writing
- involvement (in the field)
- courage to fail coupled with a sense of humor
- research input
- graduate work.

Although a long list and one that need not describe each and every author, Rainey's synthesis provides a good description of the orientation necessary for success in writing for publication.

Brodinsky (1975), writing for the Education Press of America, reviewed various authors' and editors' comments on the means by which better articles may be written. He emphasizes having good reasons for writing, selecting the appropriate medium, properly organizing the article, writing to inform rather than impress, knowing the subject matter, and working from a clear frame of reference. A list of his suggestions for better articles is included as Figure 3.

FIGURE 3:   How to Get Better Educational Articles

- Get a good topic and then get a good writer for it.
- The editor should place himself or herself in the author's shoes and the author should wear the editor's hat.
- The trouble with many educational articles is that they are simply band-wagoning a topic which has already gained fame.
- Here is one test for an article: after writing or reading it, could you quickly construct an outline and identify its major points?
- Authors should write in English.
- No magazine can depend on manuscripts coming over the transom.
- One way to get a good magazine article is to pull together material published in a book; that is, material that deals with a single point of interest to educators.
- Other tests for the quality of an article: Does the typist like it? Does the proofreader like it? Does the printer like it?
- The expert who can't write and the teacher with a good story but inability to communicate can be helped to turn out a good article. Use the tape recorder, ask questions, prod for anecdotes.
- A good manuscript shines with its use of anecdotes.
- When planning to write an article, the first thing to do is to steep yourself in the subject. Know what you're talking about.
- Don't make the mistake of thinking that this big bulk of stuff—this first draft—is an article. Start rewriting, editing, revising.
- Editors like to get manuscripts about people.
- The interview is a most useful means for getting facts, anecdotes and direct quotations for use in an article.
- Nothing will improve the quality of educational articles so much as mastering the technique of the point of view. We need not always write and publish articles written from the point of view of the "I'm the expert. . . ."

Motivation to publish is an important consideration for the author, particularly in light of the competition for a limited number of journal pages. Spithill (1973) sees lack of motivation and dedication as the primary stumbling block for authors. She indicates that failure to sustain motivation is typically the result of one of two factors: over concern about lack of skill with words and grammatical construction (although their importance is undeniable) and "compulsive perfectionism"—getting hung up on the quality of the parts to the loss of the whole.

Brodbelt (1967) speaks of the issue of the usefulness of research. He suggests that authors, when deciding to publish research, consider its utility and write in such a way that the practitioner is able to use research findings. That is, the writer should know what sort of audience is likely to be able to use his or her information and should write to make that information comprehensible.

Zirkel (1978), writing in the *Journal of Teacher Education*, provides a list of helpful hints for the prospective journal author. They are based on input from a seminar panel dealing with publication in education, which was jointly sponsored by Education Press of America and the American Association of Colleges of Teacher Education. Zirkel suggests following these hints in the order they are presented:

- read and research before you write
- select a project for which you have preparation and motivation
- build a reputation
- shop around
- always query
- collaborate with complementary colleagues
- aim at your audience
- select a style and stick with it
- make writing a habit
- let someone tough read your manuscript before submitting it
- have two other brown envelopes ready in case of rejection
- once you get cooking, don't hesitate to change the recipe.

Much of what is written about publishing in journals is specifically directed towards particular audiences or journals. Conklin (1968) addresses herself to public school teachers who wish to publish articles on classroom methods. She outlines nine steps to follow in preparing the article: what to write about, research, studying the market, outline, the query, timing, writing the article, photographs, and preparing the manuscript. Wall (1974), a copy and production editor for the *Personnel and Guidance Journal*, discusses the process of getting into print from submission to actual publication. Her experience as an editor places emphasis on clarity of writing, syntax, and word choice as a means of increasing chances for acceptance.

Wentling (1977), in an outline prepared for a workshop on journal publishing at the American Vocational Association Convention, describes the publication process in the field of vocational education. The outline includes such topics as why write, types of journals, types of articles, suggestions for getting started, publication mechanics, and suggestions from the editors. Papers of this type can be found at most professional association meetings with articles of a similar nature appearing every few years in an association's principal journal.

Several other sources (Delaney, 1969; Ohles, 1970; Roesch, 1968; Turbeville, 1967) provide overlapping pragmatic pointers for the practitioner as a potential journal author. As an antidote to editorphobia, Gilman (1978) shares a sample of rejection letters. He ends by encouraging fellow fledgling writers to take heart; articles about getting into or not getting into print show that there are many ways to get published.

EVALUATING THE ARTICLE

A systematic self-evaluation and critique of a manuscript prior to submitting it to a journal can reveal many of the shortcomings of an article draft, shortcomings an editor would certainly observe. There are sources the author can use as guides that describe what makes for a quality, publishable manuscript.

A set of criteria for assessing the publishability of an article can be derived from an article by Ward, Hall, and Schramm (1975). They distributed a questionnaire to selected members of the American Educational Research Association, asking that 114 articles in education and related fields be evaluated on 33 characteristics. Evaluation of the quality of these sample articles can serve as a checklist authors can follow in assessing their own work. A listing of these ratings appears in Table 1. In a similar survey, Frantz (1968) queried the editorial boards of six guidance and education journals. He lists three considerations that make for a quality research report: (1) identification of important problems leading to integration and extension of previous findings, (2) clear and appropriate writing of articles, and (3) research designs controlling for as many confounding variables as possible. Frantz also describes those criteria the editors viewed as most important in differentiating acceptable from unacceptable articles. The five highest were: contribution to knowledge, design of study, objectivity in reporting results, topic selection, and writing style and readability. A complete list of these 14 criteria appears in Table 2.

Mullins (1977) offers extensive recommendations and guidelines for preparing, critiquing, and adjusting scholarly manuscripts. She addresses nearly all aspects of this form of writing from clearly defining topic, scope, and context, to preparing outlines, to coding drafts, and so on. Her work is a most complete volume dealing with the various issues that can impede and facilitate writing for publication.

In an article reviewing journal selection criteria, Silverman (1978) notes a variety of reasons for rejection of manuscripts submitted. The most commonly given reasons include "poorly written," "unscholarly," "too scholarly" (obviously, extremes are to be avoided), "too much or too little emphasis on practical implications," "unsuited to readers," and "poor writing and technical quality." Editors of research journals adhere largely to one set of technical criteria including "poor research design," "weak rationale for a study," and "inadequate methodological design." The editors of scholarly journals—defined by Silverman as journals comprising both empirically derived data and practical issues—mention lack of "technical excellence" (here referring to quality

TABLE 1:   Mean Ratings of 33 Characteristics of 114 Research Articles Published in 1971

Characteristics	Education Journals, Research	Education Journals, Non-research	All Education Journals	Related-Profession Journals	All Journals
A. Title					
(1) Title is well related to content of article	3.60	3.45	3.55	4.13	3.80
B. Problem					
(2) Problem is clearly stated	3.49	2.95	3.31	3.80	3.54
(3) Hypotheses are clearly stated	2.90	2.75	2.84	2.93	2.88
(4) Problem is significant	3.28	3.38	3.31	3.78	3.52
(5) Assumptions are clearly stated	2.45	2.32	2.41	2.76	2.56
(6) Limitations of the study are stated	2.19	2.33	2.24	2.54	2.37
(7) Important terms are defined	2.94	2.70	2.86	2.86	2.86
C. Review of literature					
(8) Coverage of the literature is adequate*	3.05	2.80	2.97	3.62	3.27
(9) Review of the literature is well organized*	3.05	2.85	2.98	3.55	3.24
(10) Studies are examined critically*	2.24	2.16	2.21	2.94	2.55
(11) Source of important findings is noted*	3.18	3.16	3.18	3.84	3.48
(12) Relationship of the problem to previous research is made clear	3.03	3.00	3.02	3.82	3.39
D. Procedures					
(13) Research design is described fully	3.07	3.19	3.11	3.68	3.36
(14) Research design is appropriate to solution of the problem	2.98	2.71	2.89	3.44	3.14
(15) Research design is free of specific weaknesses	2.49	2.48	2.48	2.90	2.67
(16) Population and sample are described	3.02	3.24	3.10	3.67	3.35
(17) Method of sampling is appropriate	2.61	2.75	2.66	2.77	2.71
(18) Data gathering methods or procedures are described	3.10	3.24	3.15	3.84	3.46

(19) Data gathering methods or procedures are appropriate to the solution of the problem	2.95	2.95	2.95	3.42	3.15
(20) Data gathering methods or procedures are used correctly	3.14	3.30	3.19	3.58	3.37
(21) Validity & reliability of data gathering procedures are established	2.19	2.52	2.31	2.59	2.43
E. Data Analysis					
(22) Appropriate methods are selected to analyze data	3.20	2.95	3.12	3.46	3.27
(23) Methods utilized in analyzing the data are applied correctly	3.24	2.80	3.09	3.78	3.41
(24) Results of the analysis are presented clearly	2.91	3.05	2.95	3.43	3.17
(25) Tables and figures are effectively used*	3.23	2.70	3.05	3.12	3.08
F. Summary & Conclusions					
(26) Conclusions are clearly stated	3.38	3.20	3.32	3.56	3.43
(27) Conclusions are substantiated by the evidence presented	3.02	2.80	2.95	3.08	3.01
(28) Conclusions are relevant to the problem*	3.50	3.21	3.41	3.71	3.55
(29) Conclusions are significant*	2.90	2.88	2.89	3.00	2.94
(30) Generalizations are confined to the population from which the sample was drawn	2.49	2.80	2.59	3.06	2.80
G. Form & Style					
(31) Report is clearly written	3.14	3.76	3.35	3.67	3.49
(32) Report is logically arganized	3.32	3.43	3.36	3.80	3.56
(33) Tone of the report displays an unbiased, impartial, scientific attitude	3.29	3.43	3.33	3.82	3.55
Median	3.04	2.90	3.00	3.45	3.26

* Variables not in 1962 survey.

Note: Ratings based on a 5-point Likert scale with 5 as the highest rating. From, Ward, H.W., Hall, B.W., & Schramm, L.F. Evaluation of published educational research: A national survey. *American Educational Research Journal*, 1975, *12*, 109-128, Copyright 1975 by the American Educational Research Association. Reprinted by permission.

**TABLE 2:   Summary of 14 Criteria
for Evaluation of Manuscripts Ranked
in Importance by 55 Members of the
Editorial Boards of Six Journals**

Criteria	Mean Rank	SD
1. Contribution to knowledge	1.8	1.2
2. Design of study	3.5	2.1
3. Objectivity in reporting results	4.7	2.3
4. Topic selection	5.5	2.9
5. Writing style and readability	5.7	2.7
6. Practical implications	6.4	3.3
7. Statistical analyses	6.5	2.5
8. Theoretical model	7.0	2.7
9. Review of literature	7.2	2.3
10. Clarity of tabular material	8.1	2.3
11. Length	10.2	1.6
12. Punctuation	11.5	1.9
13. Reputation of author	12.6	1.9
14. Institutional affiliation	13.5	0.9

From Frantz, T.T. Criteria for publishable manuscripts. *Personnel and Guidance Journal*, 1968, 47,
384-386. Copyright 1968 by the American Personnel
and Guidance Association. Reprinted by permission.

of writing), "relevance to reader interest," and other stylistic matters. Apparently in all but the highly research-oriented journals,
jargon and pure research are downplayed in favor of utility and
ease of comprehension by the wider readership of these
publications.

In a relatively new and inexpensive publication, Gilbert (1977)
offers a guide, *Clear Writing*, that features a checklist of techniques
to improve style and a set of guidelines for evaluation of
manuscripts.

EXAMINING THE
ACCEPTANCE-REJECTION PROCESS

Schick (1972), founder of the *Journal of Developmental Reading,* and Kline (1972), editor of the *Journal of Reading* and

Reading Teacher, discuss the steps taken in submitting an article for consideration along with the stages in the evaluation process, the possible outcomes, and what editorial comments imply. Ohles (1970) presents similar information from the author's standpoint. Schick, Kline, and Ohles all speak of the time required for refereeing, attending to journal submission requirements (style, number of copies, return envelopes, and the like), accepting a critique as constructive criticism, and that resubmission, with indicated and recommended changes, may be appropriate and fruitful.

In a related article, Seaton (1975) reviewed publication lags and acceptance rates for 53 journals in education, comparing 1966 figures with 1972 data. Table 3 is a summary of his findings. The frequent increases in average review time, time from acceptance to publication, and decrease in acceptance rates, reflecting increasing number of submissions and decreasing number of available pages (Sculley, 1975, 1976) are notable. Information such as Seaton's may facilitate selection of a journal; however, following recommendations for how to prepare a good journal article remains the key to success.

In her *Guide to Writing and Publishing in the Social and Behavioral Sciences,* Mullins (1977) also presents a table outlining publication characteristics of over 500 journals, including estimates of publication lag times and acceptance rates. These figures are reportedly derived from information collected at about the same time Seaton gathered his data. Arnold and Doyle (1975) also include data similar in scope and time.

Rodriguez and Uhlenberg (1978) present presumably more up-to-date data about lag times and acceptance rates. Their findings, as presented in Table 4, reflect the tightening supply-demand dynamics as of 1976. However, the skewed sample, based on a response rate to their survey of less than 50 percent, makes the market look worse than it is. For example, in comparison to Seaton's findings on a journal-to-journal basis, their survey seems to show that some of the journals have moved to a higher acceptance rate.

TABLE 3: Lags and Acceptance rates for Education Journals

Education Journals	Average Review Time (weeks)		Average Time From Acceptance to Publication (weeks)		Acceptance Rates (%)	
	1966/67	1972/73	1966/67	1972/73	1966/67	1972/73
American Education	2	2	14	14	2	2
AERJ	N/A	2	24	32	N/A	5
American Secondary Education	2	4	4	20	75	50
Art Education	9	18	9	15	5	5
Behavior Research and Therapy	8	10	12	18	25	15
California Teachers Association	18	6	72	56	N/A	N/A
Childhood Education	4	4	N/A	N/A	N/A	N/A
College Composition and Communication	2	2	16	20	25	15
College and University	3	3	15	15	20	20
College and University Journal	N/A	4	N/A	14	N/A	20
Comparative Education Review	N/A	12	N/A	6	N/A	10
Contemporary Education	8	8	36	36	N/A	60
Counselor Education	6	10	36	50	50	25
Education	4	6	32	52	60	50
Educational Forum	N/A		N/A	36	N/A	5
Educational Researcher	N/A	2	N/A	8	N/A	N/A
Educational Technology	2	2	8	50	50	50
Elementary English	N/A	6	36	N/A	20	10
Elementary School Guidance and Counseling	12	14	24	20	25	20
Exceptional Children	14	14	25	9	25	15
Harvard Educational Review	6	6	N/A	12	N/A	N/A
Instructor	3	3	52	52	15	10
Journal of College Placement	6	4	10	18	70	60
Journal of Education	N/A	6	3	8	N/A	N/A
Journal of Educational Measurement	N/A	8	N/A	30	N/A	20
Journal of Experimental Analysis of Behavior	7	7	16	16	50	50
Journal of Experimental Education	4	6	52	52	50	50
Journal of General Education	4	4	40	36	N/A	N/A

TABLE 3: *(Continued)*

Education Journals	Average Review Time (weeks)		Average Time From Acceptance to Publication (weeks)		Acceptance Rates (%)	
	1966/67	*1972/73*	*1966/67*	*1972/73*	*1966/67*	*1972/73*
Journal of Higher Education	N/A	4	N/A	24	N/A	8
Journal of Learning Disabilities	N/A	8	N/A	40	N/A	25
Journal of Reading	N/A	5	N/A	24	N/A	25
Journal of Reading Behavior	6	8	32	12	75	50
Journal of Research and Development in Education	N/A	N/A	12	N/A	5	2
Journal of School Psychology	5	5	26	35	50	35
Journal of Secondary Education	3	2	13	10	5	3
Journal of Special Education	10	4	52	30	30	20
Journal of Speech and Hearing Disorders	N/A	8	N/A	18	58	50
Journal of Teacher Education	N/A	24	N/A	N/A	N/A	1
N.A.S.S.P. Bulletin	N/A	5	52	N/A	N/A	20
National Elementary Principal	20	8	52	104	23	10
Nation's Schools	4	2	N/A	N/A	N/A	N/A
North Central Association Quarterly	4	4	32	16	4	4
Pennsylvania School Journal	N/A	12	N/A	26	N/A	N/A
Phi Delta Kappan	5	6	10	12	8	5
Reading Horizons	12	8	24	52	75	75
Reading Improvement	4	6	32	52	70	40
Reading Research Quarterly	N/A	10	39	52	33	10
Reading Teacher	N/A	5	N/A	25	N/A	25
School and Community	2	2	8	12	75	25
School Counselor	26	8	52	12	N/A	20
Teachers College Record	N/A	4	N/A	28	N/A	20
Vocational Guidance	N/A	6	N/A	12	N/A	25
Means for all Journals	6.9	6.7	27.8	35.4	36.4	24.6

From Seaton, H.W. Education journals: Publication lags and acceptance rates. *Educational Researcher,* 1975, *4*(4), 18-19. Copyright 1975 by the American Educational Research Association. Reprinted by permission.

TABLE 4: Survey Summary

Educational Journals	Unsolicited Manuscripts Received	Number Accepted for Publication	Percentage of Rejections	Acceptance to Publication Time	Status as Refereed Journal
American Educational Research Journal	350	25	93%	2-3 mos.	yes
Childhood Education	20	2	90%	3-6 mos.	—
Contemporary Education	147	13	91%	6-12 mos.	yes
EdCentric Magazine	200	20	85%	3-6 mos.	—
Educational Horizons	150	5	97%	3-12 mos.	yes
Educational Studies	100	30	80%	3-9 mos.	yes
Educational Theory	235	42	82%	9-12 mos.	yes
Elementary School Journal	400	60	85%	6-12 mos.	—
Harvard Educational Review	400	20	95%	2-4 mos.	yes
Journal of Education	200	5	98%	6-8 mos.	yes
Journal of Educational Research	750	80	89%	3 mos.	yes
Journal of Research & Development in Education	75	48	36%	6 mos.	no
Journal of Teacher Education	400	27	93%	6-12 mos.	yes
Journal of Experimental Education	240	70	71%	12 mos.	yes
Learning	1,500	30	98%	6 mos.	no
National Elementary Principal	223	6	97%	1-3 mos.	no
Phi Delta Kappan	1,100	100	91%	6 mos.	NA
Today's Education	1,500	100	93%	3 mos.	—
University of Chicago School Review	305	23	92%	12 mos.	yes

From Rodriguez, R., & Uhlenberg, D.M. Publish? or perish: The thought. *Journal of Teacher Education*, 1978, *29*, 64-66. Copyright 1978 by the American Association of Colleges of Teacher Education. Reprinted by permission.

4
BOOKS AND
MONOGRAPHS

If publishing in education can be viewed in terms of a continuum, then books and monographs would be at one end, conference papers at the other end, and journal articles in the middle. Books and monographs are both quantitatively and qualitatively different from either papers or articles.

There is no single category for educational books. The textbook, the professional or scholarly book directed toward the practitioner and specialized student, and the broad market trade book vary in their content, appeal, publisher focus, and financial benefits to the author.

Textbooks—elementary, high school, and college—typically take one of two forms: the survey text, which provides an extensive review of the basic literature or content of a field, and the supplemental text, which treats a subarea in greater detail (Dessauer, 1974). The professional or scholarly book, often published by university presses as well as commercial publishers, is more specialized, summarizing research in a specialty and/or presenting new theoretical or conceptual formulations of research issues, problems, or models. Addressing a wider audience than the others are trade books such as Holt's *How Children Fail* (1964) and Herndon's *The Way It Spozed to Be* (1968). These works seek to familiarize students, professionals, and the general public with issues in the field.

Monographs, on the other hand, are works longer than articles but still typically dealing with a single narrow topic or reporting a series of studies or one major study. They are published with less concern for marketability and with greater emphasis on purely academic interests than are most books. This format is very appropriate when the material has a limited audience making it unprofitable for publishers to commit the large amounts of time and money necessary for a book's development and marketing.

The process of submitting a book for publication is different from submission procedures for a paper or an article. However, the benefits that can accrue from publication of these longer works may be worth the effort in many cases. [Centra (1977) found publication of books and monographs to be a major factor in evaluating faculty performance, especially at research universities. Tuckman (1976), however, reports only small salary gains for book publishing faculty members. Actual salary losses for some persons publishing ten or more books in their academic careers have been observed. As noted in Chapter I, Tuckman attributes this to devotion of too much time to writing at the expense of other monetarily remunerative pastimes.] Because the book publishing business is so competitive, a logical first step is to find a publisher.

FINDING A PUBLISHER

Selecting a book publisher is a different process from selecting a conference or journal. Publisher and audience are not as readily matched as they are via specialized conferences and journals. Most frequently a publisher is chosen by means of personal contacts, by publisher invitation, or by author familiarity with a given publisher's reputation. Other factors that can also influence an author's choice include the quality of a publisher's list of titles, impressions of sales personnel, reactions to editors, comprehensiveness of marketing programs, appearance of books, pricing policies, and whether books on similar topics have been published by the company (Middendorf, 1976). All these considerations are important in determining how well a book will be distributed and sold. Broad distribution is necessary to reimburse the large investment required to transform ideas into book form. Dessauer (1974) notes that about 80 percent of all professional books are generated through publisher initiative while only 20 percent result from author submission. He does not cite a source for these figures, however, so it should not dissuade one from submitting unsolicited manuscripts.

In a survey conducted by Robinson and Higbee (1978), the most frequent reasons authors gave for having selected their publishers were:

- knowing and/or liking an editor or field representative of a company
- being approached directly by a publisher
- having some notion of the publisher's reputation.

Reputation was the most frequently given reason for signing with a given publisher. This is not such a capricious reason as it might seem. Presence, visibility, and size are directly related to marketing policies. It makes sense that the larger companies are better able to promote their wares. Advertising means sales.

Listings of publishers are available but, unlike journal compendia, the information they provide is often limited to company, address, and telephone number. The best known of the directories that list book publishers is the annual *Literary Market Place*. The 1978–79 edition is the 38th annual revision of this directory of American book publishing. It is both a register of the personnel in the publishing field and a buyer's guide for the purchase of materials and service. The directory is divided into 82 sections grouped under 12 interest areas. Each entry is accompanied by an annotation that includes name, address, phone number, contact person, and other useful information.

Another very useful source for finding a publisher is *1978 Writer's Market* (Koester & Hillman, 1977). According to its editors, it is the "most comprehensive supermarket of opportunities for writers ever assembled" (their Preface). The publication is composed of seven major sections that include: introductory materials; book publishers; trade, technical, and professional journals; farm publications; company publications; consumer publications; and miscellaneous free-lance markets and services. Each section, except the introductory material, contains an annotated bibliography of information for that subject. The information includes (where appropriate) the publication or publisher's name and address, editor's name, publication emphasis, frequency of publication, readership, circulation, submission requirements, payments, and much more.

A third possible source for finding a publisher is *The Writer's Handbook,* edited by Burack. This annual publication, which was completely revised for the 1978 edition, contains four parts, one of which deals specifically with names and addresses of magazine and book publishers. This part, entitled "Writer's Market," also contains information on manuscript requirements, length, type of material wanted, and payment rates. The other three parts are also useful to the book writer and include: "Background for Writers," which offers inspiration and advice, "How to Write," which deals with specific techniques used by outstanding writers, and "Editorial and Business Side" information.

Another publication that could be useful to a prospective author in helping to select a publisher is *Books in Print.* This is an annual six-volume publication with separate author, subject, and title listings for all books published in the United States. Each entry includes author(s), title, publisher, volume and edition, Library of Congress number, date of publication, and price.

Penchansky (1974) provides an annotated bibliographic listing of directories, indices, catalogs, distributors, presses, alternative publishing opportunities, special publishing groups, and other nontraditional book publishing outlets. Publishing houses also frequently have displays at major conferences, and information may be obtained from sales representatives.

Publishing through "vanity presses" or, as one such publisher refers to his business, "subsidy publishing" (Uhlan, 1977), is a valid alternative if the author is willing and able to take the risk of not recouping his or her investment. The author pre-pays publishing costs at a rate based upon the length and content (tables, photographs, and the like) of the manuscript. For example, Exposition Press charged $5,000 for a press run of 3,000 copies of a 176 page volume (Uhlan, 1972), although these costs most certainly have risen. This kind of publishing is generally not very prestigious.

Other subsidy publishers are less deserving of the appellation "vanity press" in that they have selection and refereeing processes to eliminate unsound and poor quality works. One such organization, the University Press of America (no date), requires a minimum order (75 copies), and a board of academics and scholars provides a more selective decision process. There are, of course, publication costs, but they are less than those of, for example, Exposition Press. There is an acceptance-rejection decision, but the greater prestige accrued from the refereeing process could be worth the risks involved. In both types of cases, the bulk of the editing is left to the author, although marketing largely remains the responsibility of the publisher.

SUBMITTING A PROSPECTUS

Zeiger (1976), the academic advisor for Harper & Row publishers, describes qualities he looks for in deciding whether to recommend a book for publication. The primary criteria are a book's value and uniqueness, that is, "who needs it?" and "why is this book different from all other books?" (p. 1). These questions are raised because book publishing is a profit-oriented operation. Without some assurance of a market, a publishing house is unlikely to invest in a work. For the author to answer these questions he or she must have a familiarity with other works on the market and a sense of purpose for creating a new book. If there is a need for a given book's content or perspective, the probability of acceptance is increased markedly, particularly if the author can present this case well in the prospectus.

The prospectus is an outline of the book's contents, its objectives, intended audience, and features, plus a sample chapter or two and a copy of the author's vita or some indication of qualifications to write such a book. Van Til (1978) refers to the "holy trinity revered by textbook publishers: a query letter, a detailed outline, and a sample chapter" (p. 417). The prospectus, according to Zeiger, can make or break the author's chances for publication. Also, preparation of an outline and sample chapters for the prospectus requires that the author develop a realistic sense of the magnitude of effort required to write an entire volume. Failure to have this foreknowledge of the work involved can lead to publishers' most frequently voiced complaint about authors: they failed to complete the manuscript or meet the deadlines (Robinson & Higbee, 1978).

Middendorf (1976) emphasizes the advantages of submitting a prospectus to a specific person at a publishing house. There are problems enough with unsolicited, "over the transom" manuscripts. Compounding these problems with the salutation "To Whom it May Concern" or "Dear Editor" will not help the author. Obtaining the name of a contact person should involve no more than a telephone call or letter to a company, a brief talk with a colleague who has published a book, or consulting some of the directories described in the previous section of this chapter. Of course, "over the transom" manuscripts (i.e., manuscripts submitted in whole without a prior solicitation) are sometimes accepted, but are typically given to the least senior editor or reviewer to read and reject (Van Til, 1973). Submission of a prospectus and letter of inquiry will, most often, yield a reply that will assess the feasibility of the project, which will at least cut down the amount of unnecessary and unrewarded work to be done.

It must be emphasized that the refereeing process for a book manuscript is even more rigorous than for a journal article. The significant financial investment involved in book publishing and the reputation of publishing houses make for stringent critiquing and reviewing to insure valid selection. Initial review is by an editor or authority in the manuscript's subject field. An editorial board or committee then evaluates the prospectus or manuscript. Other viewpoints may be brought in before a decision to publish is made. A detailed and well written prospectus can facilitate this decision-making process by offering a good sample of the author's writing style and by presenting the intended scope of the work in detail.

Despite (or perhaps because of) the quality of the precontract manuscript and prospectus, the likelihood of having a book manuscript accepted for publication is relatively low. Robinson and Higbee report that of nearly 3,000 manuscripts submitted to publishers in their survey, only 5 percent (154) resulted in contracts.

NEGOTIATING THE CONTRACT

Middendorf indicates that most contracts offered to textbook authors are basically the same. He views this as justification for submitting a prospectus to only one publisher at a time. Robinson and Higbee's survey, however, revealed a variety of royalty, advance, marketing, and other contractual arrangements among publishing houses. A list of the 25 publishers in the Robinson and Higbee survey, along with their responses to questions concerning royalties, advances, cash grants, permissions, and illustrations, is presented in Table 5. They report that the most frequent royalty arrangements are either 15 percent or a sliding scale based upon sales of the textbook. Robinson and Higbee deal primarily with works produced by large profit-making companies. The royalty rate (s) , arrangements for payment for indexing, illustrations, permissions, and so forth are developed through negotiations with a publisher. The 15 percent figure is not a hard and fast one. Author reputation and past sales record, currency of the title, scholarship of the work, and other factors influence royalty rates offered an author. More important still are the nature of the work and the publishing house. Robinson and Higbee's data apply to textbooks. Dessauer (1974) describes professional book rates as typically 10 percent of the list price, 15 percent of the publisher's receipts, or as low as 5 percent on direct sales. Baumol and Heim (1967) estimate that about 60 percent of publishers base royalty rates on list price (commercial publishers, 53 percent; university presses, 67 percent). The rest utilize gross or net proceeds or some combination of the two. Sliding rates dependent upon sales are common for trade books. Paperback books are usually at a lower rate (4 to 7 percent). University presses, frequently nonprofit pub-

TABLE 5:   How Publishers Handle Monetary Issues

Publisher	(a) Royalty	(b) Advance	(c) Cash Grants	(d) Per-missions	(e) Illus-trations
Academic Press	10-15%	No	Yes-No	Au-Pub	Pub
Addison-Wesley	15%	No	Yes	Pub	Pub
Allyn and Bacon	18%	Yes	Yes-No	Pub-Au	Pub
Brooks-Cole	10-15%	Yes	No	Au	Au-Pub
C. V. Mosby	15%	Yes	No	Au	Au-Pub
Chandler	15%	No	No	Au	Pub
Dorsey Press	15%	Yes-No	No	Au-Pub	Pub
Freeman	15%	Yes	No	Pub	Pub
Harcourt, Brace	15-18%	Yes-No	No	Pub	Pub
Harper & Row	10-15%	No	No	Au-Pub	Pub
Heath	18%	No	No	Pub	Pub
Holt, Rinehart	10-20%	Yes	Yes-No	Pub-Au	Pub
Houghton, Mifflin	15-18¾ %	Yes-No	Yes-No	Pub	Pub
John Wiley & Son	10-19%	No	No	Au	Pub
Little, Brown	15%	No	No	Au	Pub
Macmillan	15%	Yes	No	Pub	Pub
McGraw-Hill	12-15%	Yes	No	Au	Pub
Oxford University Press	18-21%	Yes	No	Au-Pub	Pub
Prentice-Hall	15%	Yes	Yes-No	Au-Pub	Pub
Rand McNally	15%	Yes	No	Pub	Pub
Research Press	12-13%	No	No	Au	Pub
Ronald Press	15%	Yes	No	Au	Pub
Scott, Foresman	8-17%	Yes-No	No	Pub	Pub
W. A. Benjamin	8-10%	No	No	Au	Pub
W. C. Brown	15-18¾ %	Yes-No	No	Pub	Pub-Au

From Robinson, P.W., & Higbee, K.L. Publishing a textbook: Advice from authors and publishers. *Teaching of Psychology,* 1978, *5,* 175-181. Copyright 1978 by Division Two of the American Psychological Association. Reprinted by permission of the authors and the journal editor.

lishers, must offer generally lower rates than commercial publishers.

The respondents to Robinson and Higbee's survey suggest various means by which an author can gain a clearer understanding of the contractual process. They emphasize obtaining advice from a third party—an attorney or someone experienced with such matters. Other suggestions include comparing contracts (should more than one be offered), checking contract details and promotion information, and having every aspect of the agreement in writing. These suggestions treat the author as just what he or she is, a consumer of publishing services. If one is willing to spend the time comparative shopping for groceries, even more time ought to be spent evaluating publishers and examining contracts.

In their very comprehensive article in the *AAUP Bulletin*, Baumol and Heim (1967) discuss the process of contracting with a book publisher and report the results of a survey responded to by 350 faculty who had previously published a book. They report that standard financial arrangements take four main forms:

- royalty agreements
- sale of rights agreements
- stock-option agreements
- subsidy publishing agreements.

Among the four types of agreements, those based on royalties are the most common with royalty rates based upon either list price, gross or net proceeds, or some combination of the two. The sale-of-rights agreement involves the author assigning to the publisher all rights and interests in his work in return for a given sum. Stock-option agreements utilize stock in the publishing house as payment for a book, an infrequently utilized arrangement. Subsidy agreements involve payment by the author to facilitate publication, with a subsequent increase in royalty rate.

Typical contracts also include such considerations as cash advances, control of rights to quote, abridge, and reproduce, free copies and cost of additional copies to author(s), cost for corrections, and options for the publisher to publish subsequent writings. Baumol and Heim also point out that the contract itself is rarely a commitment on the part of the publisher to publish but does bind the author to the publisher. A complete reading of this article is recommended for anyone approaching book publication for the first time.

Barber (1975), an author and literary agent, offers guidelines to authors negotiating contracts with publishers. She indicates that it is not necessary to accept without question the contents of a proffered contract. Barber discusses definitions of manuscript acceptability (the publisher's "escape clause"), rights to print and distribute, warranties that are ill-defined (e.g., "obscene or scandalous"), indemnities, payments and royalties, advances, subsidiary rights and income, options for subsequent books, and termination clauses as aspects of contracts needing careful examination. She recommends that authors obtain an inexpensive bibliography on book contracts and a sample contract from the Authors Guild (234 West 44th Street, New York, New York, 10019). Mullins (1977) also offers a section dealing with contract negotiation, largely consistent with Barber's recommendations.

WRITING THE MANUSCRIPT

Writing a book requires a great deal of time and work. This understatement is borne out by Robinson and Higbee's (1978) report that the modal time taken to write a book is two years. Fully one-tenth of all authors responding to their survey took more than five years to complete their manuscripts. The respondents' most frequently given advice to new authors is, "It will take more time than planned" (p. 9). In fact, it will often take about twice as long, and even after the manuscript is complete, there is much more to be done.

The demands involved in actually writing a book vary as to content, the author's writing facility, available time, and amount of research required. To simplify the writing-editing process, however, many publishing houses frequently provide writer's guides to persons under contract (Barcombe, 1974). These guides describe the technicalities of manuscript preparation and organization as preferred by that particular publisher. An extensive discussion of procedures for preparing and submitting a manuscript is provided in Chapter VI, Style Manuals and Writing Guides, in this text. For inspiration and advice on the more creative aspects of writing, many books are available and none are reviewed here. However, the introductory section of *1978 Writers Market* and the first two parts of *The Writer's Handbook,* which were reviewed previously in this chapter, should be useful to prospective book authors.

Zeiger (1976) discusses the balances an author must strike in preparing a manuscript. The author must "find a middle ground between originality and eccentricity" (p. 4). That is, the book must be different, but not too different. Being too different can detract from the book's usefulness. A compromise must be made when writing for the various populations in the intended audience. Too scholarly a presentation could affect the book's marketability. Also, a consistent and clearly presented frame of reference is necessary, incorporating both the orientation and goals of the book and author in such a way as to give the text continuity and flow.

At this stage in the book writing process, contact between author and editor is critical. Completion of the manuscript, preparation of the index, tables, and graphs, selection and placement of illustrations, and obtaining permission to utilize others' materials are all part of the author's interaction with the editor. Publication schedules are arranged months in advance, so sticking to deadlines is very important. Printing and proofreading schedules are tight due to printers' workloads; therefore, failure to meet a deadline at a given stage (galleys, page proofs) can result in the printer taking the work off the line, expensively delaying the publication process by perhaps one to two months. The publishers in Robinson and Higbee's (1976) survey report that, for most cases of delay, there were no good reasons. Should the author anticipate an additional book to follow, his or her cooperation on earlier works would help insure continued acceptance and cooperation.

PUBLISHING THE MANUSCRIPT
AS A MONOGRAPH

The monograph is a special case of the book length manuscript. Here, the financial issues are not paramount. The refereeing process is as selective but centers less on the attractiveness and marketability of the work than on the reason for existence of the manuscript idea in longer form and on the rigor or research of the author. Kimble (1964), then editor of *Psychological Monographs,* has discussed the policies, procedures, and expectations of *Psychological Monographs.* The information is equally applicable to other monograph publishers. Kimble indicates that there are two kinds of acceptable products for *Psychological Monographs*: (1) a series of related studies leading to some kind of theoretical closure and (2) a single, intensive study, sometimes in a new area of research, which requires considerable development of theoretical and historical background, detailed interpretive analysis, or both. Kimble states that the monograph, as a self-contained unit, demands seven well-developed features:

- adequate historical and theoretical background development
- definitions of theoretical terms and theoretical vocabulary
- description of procedures in more detail than in journal articles
- instructions to subjects to illustrate procedures
- important items from questionnaires and descriptions of scoring methods
- statistical and other analyses in detail
- substantial summary.

Quality, format, and length of manuscript are also of import. Kimble complains that too often manuscripts submitted are little more than wordy articles that can readily be reduced in size or dissertations that were not worth shortening for publication elsewhere. Mullins (1977) suggests section lengths consistent with the purpose of the monograph form of in-depth analysis. She recommends a 10-page introductory chapter, a 50-page literature review, and several chapters of findings and discussion.

In an old but still useful article, Conrad (1948) presents a step-by-step guide to organizing a monograph. He addresses himself to 26 subjects, including double-spacing, table of contents, punctuation, estimates of printed pages, and so on. The information covered in "Style Manuals and Writing Guides," Chapter VI of this text, applies here also.

By following Kimble's definitions and descriptions and paying attention to the details in Conrad's article, an author may find some of the uncertainty removed from the mechanics of monograph preparation. While acceptance is not guaranteed (a bad work, no matter how well prepared, remains a bad work), the author who follows these guidelines can at least have some certainty that his or her work is prepared according to accepted monograph style.

5
INDICES

The literature review is basic to all forms of publication, whether it be reporting basic research, synthesizing past works, or developing totally new and creative ideas. Without a thorough review of the literature, there is no way either the author or the reader can bring a context to the work. Frantz (1968), in his review of criteria used by counseling and educational journal editors for evaluating manuscripts, indicates that a good literature review is one of the three main features of an acceptable paper. Ward, Hall, and Schramm (1975) in their summary of evaluations of journal articles find that literature reviews are among the more neglected sections of educational research. George Schick (1972), founder of the *Journal of Developmental Reading,* also emphasizes the importance of a good review to the editorial decision-making process. Familiarity with the issues and problems in research and practice, accomplished via the literature review, helps make research designs more practical and usable and less pontificating (Brodbelt, 1967).

The entry points for research reviews are the indices, abstracts, and related services. Thus, a discussion of these information sources is provided here.

COMPREHENSIVE EDUCATION INDICES

There are three on-going index-abstract services that are addressed to all areas of education: *Resources in Education, Current Index to Journals in Education,* and *Education Index.* The first two of these indices are keyed to the Education Resources Information Center (ERIC) abstracting and access system. All of them are readily available in most college and university libraries; however, not all libraries have the microfiche copies of the actual manuscripts listed in the indices.

Resources in Education

Resources in Education (RIE), which was called *Research in Education* prior to 1975, is the index to the ERIC document holdings. RIE is a monthly publication covering articles, books, monographs, and other materials received by the various ERIC clearinghouses (see Appendix B for the complete list of names and addresses for all ERIC clearinghouses). It is the abstract source most frequently utilized by AERA members in their research (Nelson, 1974).

RIE is divided into two major sections: Documents and Indices. The Document Section is organized by ERIC ED and clearinghouse accessions numbers, presenting author, title, author's affiliation, publication date, manuscript length, and price for reproduction by the ERIC Document Reproduction Service. The Index section is divided into three parts. The Subject Index lists document titles and ED accession numbers under ERIC descriptors. The Author Index lists titles and ED numbers under author names. The Institution Index is organized by agency of author affiliation. There is also cross-referencing between clearinghouse accession number and ERIC document number.

Current Index to Journals in Education

Current Index to Journals in Education (CIJE) is a semi-annual publication covering the previous half-year's articles in over 700 education and education-related journals. It was created in 1969 as a complement to RIE, which does not abstract journal articles. ERIC EJ accession numbers are assigned to articles as they are abstracted, facilitating computer abstract searches. Articles are abstracted and indexed by the ERIC clearinghouses.

CIJE is divided into four sections: Main Entry, Subject Index, Author Index, and Journal Content Index. The Main Entry section is organized by EJ number and provides a clearinghouse accession number, article title, author, journal information, descriptors under which the article is indexed and, in many cases, an abstract of the article. The Subject Index is an alphabetical listing of ERIC descriptors of subjects. Article title, journal information, and EJ number are given. The Author Index lists each author's output for the year with EJ accession numbers. The Journal Contents Index is arranged by journal title and date and lists article titles and EJ numbers. CIJE annually cites over 65,000 articles.

Both RIE and CIJE subject indices use descriptors from the *Thesaurus of ERIC Descriptors* (1980), which is updated monthly in RIE. The Thesaurus provides main, broader, narrowed, and related terms for subjects. It also includes five other sections: Descriptors, Rotated Descriptor Display, Descriptor Groups, Descriptor Group Display, and Hierarchical Display.

Education Index

Education Index (EI) is a monthly index by authors and subjects of over 250 journals, conference proceedings, bulletins, monographs, yearbooks, and United States government materials in education and related fields. Periodicals chosen for inclusion are selected by subscriber vote, so EI is not as extensive or comprehensive as CIJE. Article information is presented for each subject, author, or agency heading. Abstracts are not provided. Major advantages of EI are its frequent publication and availability in many local and community libraries, making for ready access and ease of use.

RELATED NONEDUCATION INDICES

As a result of an extensive study, Narin and Garside (1972) report that the vast majority of articles in 79 education and special education journals cite psychology journals as their major references. Because of this fact, index and abstract systems not directly related to the field of education would seem to be as valuable an asset as CIJE and EI for conducting literature reviews.

Psychological Abstracts

The noneducation index most frequently used by educators (Nelson, 1974) is *Psychological Abstracts* (PA). It is a monthly publication with a semi-annual index and abstracts over 800 periodicals, books, monographs, reports, proceedings, and dissertations in psychology and related fields. The PA index orders paper topics and index numbers within alphabetically arranged descriptors. The abstracts themselves are sequenced by number under major subject headings. Dissertations are listed with reference to *Dissertation Abstracts International* but are not abstracted. Subject headings and descriptors are reproduced and cross-indexed in the *Thesaurus of Psychological Index Terms* (APA, 1977).

Adjuncts to PA are the *Cumulative Subject Index to Psychological Abstracts* (APA, 1975b) and the *Cumulative Author Index to Psychological Abstracts* (APA, 1975a). These list articles by *Thesaurus of Psychological Index Terms* and by author respectively. Five volumes of each have been produced as of this writing: 1927–1960, 1961–1965, 1966–1968 (all published by G. K. Hall & Co.), 1969–1971, and 1972–1974 (published by APA).

Social Science Citation Index

The *Social Science Citation Index* (SSCI) is a multifocus index regularly covering over 1,000 journals in 26 disciplines and selectively reviewing 2,000 more. There are 130 journals listed under the category of "Education and Education Research." SSCI is composed of three volumes: the *Citation Index,* the *Source Index,* and the *Permuterm Subject Index.* The *Citation Index* is organized alphabetically by individual and corporate authors. It provides lists of articles the authors have published in the abstracted journals. Under each article is a list of authors and journal titles that cite the articles in their reference lists in that index year. The *Citation Index* makes it possible to trace a line of research conducted in a particular area over a period of time. The *Source Index* is an author index for SSCI of the articles published in that year. The reference list from each article is provided. The *Permuterm Subject Index* is a permuted title-word index to journals processed for SSCI. This is designed to assist the researcher in determining what authors have written articles in a given subject area for the year. Additionally SSCI produces a *Yearly Guide and Journal List,* which is a guide to using SSCI with a list of the journals indexed.

Social Sciences Index

The *Social Sciences Index* is a yearly index of over 250 journals in the social sciences with articles arranged by subject and author, much like its sister publication, *Education Index. Social Sciences Index* supersedes the *Social Sciences and Humanities Index,* 1965–1974, and the *International Index,* 1907–1965.

Sociology of Education Abstracts

Sociology of Education Abstracts is a quarterly index to over 170 periodicals, documents, books, and reports from the United States and other countries. Each article's contents are described in a detailed abstract. This resource is limited to journals dealing with social and group processes relating to education.

Current Contents in Social and Behavioral Sciences

Current Contents in Social and Behavioral Sciences is a weekly collection of reproductions of journal tables of contents. Each issue indicates in which volume a complete list of journals included appears.

MISCELLANEOUS OTHER RESOURCES

There are many other indices available that are more specific in scope (*e.g., Exceptional Child Abstracts, Educational Administration Abstracts, State Education Journal Index, Mental Retardation Abstracts, Language and Language Behavior Abstracts, British Education Index, Resources in Vocational Education, Sociology of Education: A Guide to Information Sources,* and so on). These indices are sufficiently limited in scope that elaboration, beyond mention, is not useful here; however, they are extremely valuable within the particular fields they represent.

If a person is researching an unfamiliar field, there are resources available to help. Reviewing abstracts and articles may stimulate ideas. Tracing research topics through SSCI may reveal areas of study not previously investigated. For those who still need assistance in finding ideas, Glueck and Jauch (1975) discuss the major sources of research ideas as stated by "160 productive hard science researchers" (p. 103). They indicate that the four most important sources are: the researcher him or herself, the literature, professional peers from other institutions, and local colleagues.

It is possible to find most of these indices in any academic library. Instructions for the use of each are typically provided by the index publisher, or assistance may be obtained from a reference librarian. Subject and topic selection may be clarified and refined by using the thesauri available or, again, the reference librarian may help. Locating journals may be a more difficult task, given the all too frequently limited holdings of many libraries. The Library of Congress, however, publishes the on-going *New Serial Titles: A Union List of Serials Commencing Publication after December 31, 1949,* which lists journals from the United States and abroad and at which libraries these periodicals may be found. Also, *Books in Print,* reviewed previously in Chapter IV, contains a complete listing of all books published in the United States and should be helpful in finding information published in books as opposed to journal form. Most libraries have both of these publications.

6
STYLE MANUALS
AND WRITING GUIDES

It is difficult to be certain that a manuscript is well-prepared in terms of the quality of the analysis of data, presentation of the literature review, contribution to the field, and the other factors described previously. These are subjective matters, and evaluations of their quality will vary among authors and readers. There are, however, relatively objective criteria of quality. These criteria pertain to adherence to style and to rules of good writing. Documentation, organization, sentence construction, and use of language may be compared with standards so an author can readily know the "correctness" of the manuscript in this sense. Good style will not change the written sow's ear into the proverbial silk purse, but at least a properly prepared manuscript will not be rejected out-of-hand for failure to conform to an acceptable style format. Adherence to format and writing rules will improve the "face validity" of a manuscript.

Using a clear and consistent format and following writing rules are not simply means of keeping compulsive editors busy and happy. Precision in citation, documentation, organization, word choice, and sentence construction makes for clear communication. Communication of information is the reason for the existence of conferences, papers, journals, books, and so forth. If it is not possible to understand what an author is trying to say because of unclear organization, language, or writing style, then the information is useless. The scientific method, as applied to educational research, greatly depends upon analysis of past studies. Without consistency and clarity of writing, theory development and application are not possible.

Rules for manuscript preparation, writing, and format have been developed to make for clear communication. Although forms vary—there are no right rules for style just as there are no right rules for etiquette—they all serve the ends of consistency and clarity of communication. Similarly, there are no absolutes of sentence construction, word choice, and organization of ideas, but there are resources to use that present guides for an author to follow.

STYLE MANUALS

A review of the education section of the *Directory of Publishing Opportunities* (DPO) reveals that of the 198 journals listed, most of those specifying a certain style guide require one of the following three: American Psychological Association (1974), University of Chicago Press (1969), or Modern Language Association (1977). Many of the "see latest issues for style requirements" journals also utilize one of these three. For example, the *Journal of Verbal Learning and Verbal Behavior* uses the APA format. An awareness of these three style forms is particularly helpful to paper, journal, and book authors. Although it is not within the scope of this text to present in full the American Psychological Association (APA), University of Chicago Press (Chicago), and Modern Language Association (MLA) style guides, an overview of these sources is included. Most libraries have these three style guides available for more detailed examination and use.

Many other style manuals exist; however, they all incorporate elements of the three basic guides. Some are directed towards particular types of writing. For example, *A Manual for Writers of Term Papers, Theses, and Dissertations* (Turabian, 1967) is based on Chicago and directed towards undergraduate and graduate writing. A similar guide, *Form and Style: Theses, Reports, Term Papers* (Campbell & Ballou, 1974) provides examples of all three principal formats along with much other useful information for the student writer. *A Simplified Style Manual: For Preparation of Journal Articles in Psychology, Social Sciences, Education & Literature* (Linton, 1972) is directed particularly to journals as the title indicates and utilizes primarily APA format and style. Other specific style manuals and guides include: *A Manual for Authors of Mathematical Papers* (American Mathematical Society, 1962), *The Associated Press Stylebook* (Associated Press Managing Editors Association, 1977), *U.S. News and World Report Stylebook for Writers and Editors* (U.S. News and World Report, Inc., 1977), *NEA Style Manual for Writers and Editors* (National Education Association of the United States, 1966), and *U.S. Government Printing Office Style Manual,* revised edition (U.S. Government Printing Office, 1973).

Determination of the style guide to be used should be made before preparing the manuscript. Papers are usually flexible about citation format since they are often meant to be read aloud. Journals will usually indicate which format is to be used. Book publishers may also prefer a particular style; however, internal consistency of style is more important than choice of format. The APA *Publication Manual* (1974) presents a list of non-APA journals that utilize its format. Journal compendia, such as DPO, also frequently indicate style requirements.

Publication Manual of the American Psychological Association

APA style is the most commonly used of the formats specified under "Education" in the DPO. The APA *Publication Manual* presents a highly organized system of preparing manuscripts, especially for reporting research in journals. APA format requires that a manuscript be written in a number of discrete sections: title, abstract, introduction, method, results, discussion, references, and appendix.

Parts of the Manuscript   The title is frequently the source of information on article content in indices. To make the article easily accessible, the title should be clear, informative, and brief. APA recommends no more than 12–15 words and states that "the title should summarize the main idea of the paper simply and . . . be a concise statement of the main topic and should refer to the major variables or theoretical issues . . . investigated" (p. 14).

The abstract is a brief summary of the article, replacing the concluding summary in many journals. The abstract is also used by index and abstract services. Included here should be statements of the "problem, method, results, and conclusions . . . subject population, research design, test instruments, research apparatus . . . (statistical) findings, . . . inferences made or comparisons drawn from the results" (p. 15). Reviews and theoretical articles should state "the topics covered, the central thesis, the sources used, and the conclusions drawn" (p. 15). APA recommends a 100–175 word range for abstracts of research papers, 75–100 words for reviews and theoretical articles.

The purpose of the introduction is to discuss the problem involved and the theoretical rationale for performing the investigation or writing about the topic. The literature discussion is contained in the introduction, emphasizing major conclusions, issues, and previous findings as directly relevant to the research or topic at hand. Citation of sources is required (see Citations in Text below). The introduction should also include a statement of the research problem or topic of discussion, definitions of variables, and a statement of and rationales for the hypotheses of the study, if there are any.

The fourth discrete section of the APA-organized manuscript is the method, a statement of how the study was conducted. The

APA *Publication Manual* suggests subdivisions of subjects, apparatus or materials, and procedure. If included in the paper, instructions to subjects should be included here. For nonresearch topics, much of this section would not be appropriate.

After collecting and summarizing the data, they should be presented in the results section. Tables and graphs are included here. Statistical treatments and outcomes are reported in results, without a discussion of implications beyond reporting significance levels. The APA *Publication Manual* presents detailed instructions for the preparation of tables, graphs, and figures. Again, manuscripts that do not directly deal with data-based results may need to modify this section accordingly.

Analysis of the data and their implications for the research are included in the discussion. Consequences of the research, comparison between the present and previous studies, practical implications from the data, and recommendations for future research are included here.

APA references include only those sources cited in the text. It is not a list of suggested readings. There is a specific format to be followed in arranging author, titles, and publishing information (see Reference Format).

The appendix, if there is one, should be limited to detailed descriptions or reproductions of information inappropriate to the main body. Appendices are not encouraged by APA. Items that are not useful for evaluating or understanding the research or not necessary for replication of a study should not be included. Most journal articles have no appendix, although papers, books, and monographs often do.

Citations in Text   All contributions to the research or topic are cited. Citations are given in parentheses by author or authors and date and refer to the final reference list in the work. If the author's name is included in the narrative, only the date is parenthesized. Multiple citations of the same author are arranged in chronological order. The same rule applies to corporate authors. In the absence of an author, the first two or three words from the article title in the reference list are used. Examples are:

Smith (1976) investigated open classrooms . . .
In a study of slow learners (Wilson & Jones, 1976) . . .
Brown, White, and Johnson (1975) . . . [first occurrence]
Brown, et al. (1975) . . . [subsequent occurrence]
Smith (1949, 1956, 1971a, 1971b, 1977) found . . .
Office of Education (1976)
A recent review ("The Open Classroom," 1977) . . .

Quotations should be cited as to source and page [e.g., "madness is selective . . ." (Walsh, 1975, p. 264)]. More extensive quotations should be set off in a block, the author is cited in the body of the narrative (or along with the page number), and the page number is given following the quotation. APA policy is that up to 500 words of text may be utilized without seeking permission from the copyright holder. For longer quotes, written permission is necessary. Such permission is also required if others' tables or figures are used in an article, and credit to the author and copyright holder must be included below the reproduction.

Reference Format   The reference list is composed exclusively of sources cited in the text of the manuscript. The organization of information occurs in the following order:

Author (s) surname (s) and initials in inverted order. Editors receive the parenthetical (Ed.) or (Eds.) .

Title of the article, chapter, or book. Only the first letter of the title and subsequent proper names are capitalized. Article titles are not italicized; conference papers and book titles are italicized.

Title of the journal. Initial letters of all major words are capitalized. Journal titles are italicized.

Facts of publication:

Journals: Date of publication, volume number (italicized), inclusive pages.

Books: City of publication, publisher's name, publication date.

Examples, using proper punctuation are:

Author, A. B. Article title. *Journal of Writing,* 1977, *42,* 16–31.

Author, A. B., & Writer, C. D. Article title. *Journal of Writing,* 1977, *42,* 32–65.

Author, A. B., *A book title* (2nd ed.). New York: Publishing House, 1977.

Author, A. B., Writer, C. D., & Thinker, E. F. (Eds.). *Another book.* New York: Publishing House, 1977.

References are organized alphabetically. Should there be more than one citation for an author, the titles are sequenced chronologically. More than one citation for an author in a given year should include lower case letters following the date to facilitate identifying which source is cited where in the text. Single authorship, alphabetically, precedes multiple authorship. For example:

Author, A. B. Writing articles. *Journal of Writing,* 1974, *39,* 20–24

Author, A. B. Writing other articles. *Journal of Writing,* 1975, *40,* 102–118.

Author, A. B., Writer, C. D. On collaboration. *Journal of Writing,* 1970, *35,* 80–92.

Author, A. B., Writer, C. D., & Thinker, E. F. The pitfalls of multiple authorship. *Journal of Writing,* 1971, *36,* 204–214.

Writer, C. D. Scientific writing. *Journal of Science Literature,* 1974, *21,* 18–26 (a).

Writer, C. D. Who writes? *Journal of Writing,* 1974, *39,* 138–142 (b).

For less common cases, refer to the APA *Publication Manual.*

Manual of Style of the University of Chicago Press

This frequently used style manual organizes the manuscript less precisely than does the APA *Publication Manual.* Detailed descriptions of referencing, grammatical rules and forms, tabulation, and indexing are provided. Chicago is a more book-oriented manual, while the APA manual is more article-oriented.

Parts of the Manuscript Chicago divides a manuscript into three loosely defined sections: the preliminaries, the text, and reference matter. The first defines titles, announcements, frontispiece, title page, publishing information, dedication, foreword, preface, acknowledgement, tables of contents, lists of illustrations and tables, and introduction (page assignments for each are given). The text follows whatever form is appropriate for the given manuscript, divided into chapters. The emphasis is on proper presentation of the narrative. Reference matter includes the appendix, notes, glossary, bibliography, and index. Rules for preparation of these sections are given. Where APA indicates that the reference list is the source for information cited, Chicago uses footnotes or chapter notes, with the bibliography being source and reading material. Each has a separate citation form.

Citations in Text   Textual citations are accomplished via notes (at the end of the manuscript) or footnotes (at the bottom of a page). A suprascript number refers to the note. Organization of the note is as follows:

Author's name in forward order.

Title of article in quotation marks or title of book in italics (all major words capitalized).

Facts of publication.

Where APA uses initials for given names, Chicago uses the full first name. When there are more than three authors, *et al.* may replace the names of the secondary authors. Article titles are placed in quotation marks. Unlike APA, all major words are capitalized. Book and journal titles are similarly in capitals and are italicized. Journal publication information is arranged by volume number (in Arabic; page numbers for each are given), year of publication in parentheses, and inclusive page numbers. The issue number follows the volume number when the journal has discontinuous pagination. Books are described with place of publication, publisher, and year of publication, all within parentheses. Page numbers follow the parentheses. In the Chicago format, the note numbers are not suprascript, and all information is aligned below the number.

Shortened notation may be used following the initial citation of a source. Although *op. cit.* and *loc. cit.* have been generally eliminated, *ibid.* may still be used to refer to a single work cited in the note directly preceding a citation. A shortened reference form typically uses the (primary) author's last name, some key words from the title of the work, and page numbers. Examples of a note sequence are:

1. Arnold B. Author, "Article Title," *Journal of Writing* 42 (1977) : 16–31.
2. Ibid., p. 24.
3. Arnold B. Author et al., "Article Title," *Journal of Writing* 42 (1977) : 130–150.
4. Charles D. Writer, *A New Book* (New York: Publisher, 1975), pp. 200–204.
Author et al., "Short Title," p. 147.

Reference Format   With the Chicago style, a bibliography replaces the reference section and includes both cited and recommended sources. Like APA, the list is alphabetized by last name of the primary author or manuscript title when no author is cited. If the title is used, it is placed in the list alphabetically by the first major word of the title. Although the 12th edition of the Chicago *Manual of Style* does not refer to this topic, the 11th edition (1949) indicates that, should an author be cited more than once, a three space dash is used instead of the author's name.

The sequence for articles is:

Full author name in inverted form or article title.
Title of article in quotes with major words capitalized.
Journal title italicized with first word and all major words
   capitalized.
Volume number.
Year of publication in parentheses.
Inclusive page numbers.

Book information is sequenced in the following manner:

Full author name in inverted form or book title.
Book title italicized with first word and all major words
   capitalized.
Place of publication, publisher, and year of publication, all
   within parentheses.

In the Chicago format, the secondary lines of a reference are indented, and only journal publication dates are set off by parentheses. Examples of the Chicago bibliography format are:

Author, Arnold B., "Article Title," *Journal of Writing* 42 (1977): 16–31.

———— and Writer, Charles D., "Article Title," *Journal of Writing* 42 (1977) : 32–65.

The Perfect Book (New York: Publishing Institute, 1977) .

Writer, Charles D., *A Book Title* (New York: Publishing House, 1977) .

Chicago also makes provision for citation and reference of scientific works. The forms of these are very much like APA. Internal citation is by author and date [e.g., (Author, 1977)]. Reference lists are composed of sources cited in the text. As in APA, capitals are only used for the first word of the title; secondary lines are indented; and multiple entries are listed by date as in the following examples:

Chemist, R. 1977. *The joy of chemistry.* Philadelphia: Scientific Publishers.

Psychologist, S. F.

1974. Interpersonal staff. *Journal of People* 44: 101–109.

1975. More interpersonal staff. *Journal of People* 45: 224–237.

1977. Last interpersonal staff. *Journal of People* 47: 130–147.

Modern Language Association Handbook

The format of the Modern Language Association, the *MLA Handbook* (1977) , is the third major style guide. As with Chicago, specific sectioning of a manuscript is not prescribed. The *MLA Handbook* does offer instruction on footnotes and bibliography preparation, treating them much the same as does Chicago.

Parts of the Manuscript   MLA does not describe any particular manuscript organization. The emphasis instead is on natural divisions within the work (paragraphs, quotes, and the like) . If the manuscript requires subdivisions, then major headings and subheadings are used. A division between treatment of text and notes and references is implied.

Citations in Text   Citations of sources and comments on the text are performed via footnotes or endnotes, although such commentary is not encouraged. A suprascript number or symbol that refers to the note may be located at the bottom of the page or with other notes at the end of a chapter or text. Organization of the note is as follows:

Full author's name in regular order (for single or multiple authors).
Title of article in quotation marks or title of book in italics (all major words are capitalized).
Facts of publication.

When journals are cited, the journal title with all major words in capitals is italicized, followed by volume number, date in parentheses, and inclusive pages. For books, the place of publication, publisher, and date of publication are in parentheses. Page numbers are placed at the end. Subsequent references use author's last name, short title if the author is cited more than once, and page number. *Ibid., op. cit.,* and *loc. cit.* are not used. A quadruple space is used between text and first note. Examples of the MLA style are:

[1]Arnold B. Author, "Article Title," *Journal of Writing,* 42 (1977), 16–31.
[2]Arnold B. Author and Charles D. Writer, "Article Title," *Journal of Writing,* 42 (1977), 32–65.
[3]Charles D. Writer, *A Book Title of Some Length* (New York: Publishing House, 1977), p. 350.
[4]Author, "Short Article Title," p. 30.

Reference Format   The bibliography entry format is similar to the footnotes. Entries are alphabetized. Dashes may *not* replace repeated author names. The main differences are that the author's names are inverted, page numbers in books are not included, and there are no parentheses around the book publication information. For example:

Author, Arnold B. "Article Title." *Journal of Writing,* 42 (1977), 16–31.

Writer, Charles D. *A Book Title.* New York: Publishing House, 1977.

GUIDELINES FOR NONSEXIST AND NONRACIST USE OF LANGUAGE

Discrimination based on gender is being removed from our language. Cooperation by authors, publishers, and editors is needed to reduce the effects of language on thinking in order that prejudice against and between the sexes may be eliminated. Various groups have prepared guidelines outlining the means by which authors can write in a nonsexist manner. The American Psychological Association (APA Task Force on Issues of Sexual Bias in Graduate Education, 1975), the McGraw-Hill Book Company (no date), Random House (1975), Macmillan (1975), and others have published such guidelines. The APA guide has been reproduced in at least two journals of other organizations (*American Personnel and Guidance Journal,* February 1978, and the *American Educational Research Journal,* March 1978) and is provided in Appendix D of this book. Some of these guides address racial as well as sexual stereotyping of language (e.g., Macmillan, Random House).

WRITING GUIDES

Most of the previously described style guides also address writing style, form, and content. They have sections that provide rules for punctuation, capitalization, use of quotations, use of proper names, titles, spelling, mathematics in type, abbreviations, and so on. The University of Chicago Press's *Manual of Style* contains more of this information and more examples than do the APA and MLA style manuals. Turabian (1967) includes a chapter on rules of punctuation. All these manuals also present guides for typing, mechanical preparation of manuscripts, and copy editing, although these matters are not their primary concern. Guides that are addressed primarily to writing content are also available, and several of the more prominent are reviewed here.

The Elements of Style

The most renowned of all writing guides is Strunk and White's *The Elements of Style* (1979). This brief, but information-packed, volume is one that should be useful to every writer; it is available in both cloth and paperback editions. In concise form, 11 rules of usage, 11 principles of composition, 11 matters of form, numerous words and expressions commonly misused, and 21 reminders of style are presented. The table of contents (Figure 4) alone can serve the writer admirably since William Strunk, Jr.'s rules are delineated there, without E. B. White's elaborations and examples, which appear in the text. The pleasure of *The Elements of Style* lies in its conciseness and genuine caring for the English language as it can be written.

FIGURE 4:   Table of Contents from *The Elements of Style*

I. ELEMENTARY RULES OF USAGE

1. Form the possessive singular of nouns by adding 's
2. In a series of three or more terms with a single conjunction, use a comma after each term except the last
3. Enclose parenthetic expressions between commas
4. Place a comma before a conjunction introducing an independent clause
5. Do not join independent clauses by a comma
6. Do not break sentences in two
7. Use a colon after an independent clause to introduce a list of particulars, an appositive, an amplification, or an illustrative quotation
8. Use a dash to set off an abrupt break or interruption and to announce a long appositive or summary
9. The number of the subject determines the number of the verb
10. Use the proper case of pronoun
11. A participial phrase at the beginning of a sentence must refer to the grammatical subject

II. ELEMENTARY PRINCIPLES OF COMPOSITION

12. Choose a suitable design and hold to it

13. Make the paragraph the unit of composition
14. Use the active voice
15. Put statements in positive form
16. Use definite, specific, concrete language
17. Omit needless words
18. Avoid a succession of loose sentences
19. Express co-ordinate ideas in similar form
20. Keep related words together
21. In summaries, keep to one tense
22. Place the emphatic words of a sentence at the end

III. A FEW MATTERS OF FORM

IV. WORDS AND EXPRESSIONS COMMONLY MISUSED

V. AN APPROACH TO STYLE
(With a List of Reminders)

1. Place yourself in the background
2. Write in a way that comes naturally
3. Work from a suitable design
4. Write with nouns and verbs
5. Revise and rewrite
6. Do not overwrite
7. Do not overstate
8. Avoid the use of qualifiers
9. Do not affect a breezy manner
10. Use orthodox spelling
11. Do not explain too much
12. Do not construct awkward adverbs
13. Make sure the reader knows who is speaking
14. Avoid fancy words
15. Do not use dialect unless your ear is good
16. Be clear
17. Do not inject opinion
18. Use figures of speech sparingly
19. Do not take shortcuts at the cost of clarity
20. Avoid foreign languages
21. Prefer the standard to the offbeat

A Handbook for Scholars

A recent volume that has drawn much attention from the media is van Leunen's (1978a) *A Handbook for Scholars*. Besides offering what she describes as a "new style of citation," van Leunen makes a plea for good, simple, parsimonious, comprehensible writing of scholarly literature. She offers many examples of usage, both good and bad, and discusses how references and citations may be made meaningful. The new style of citation, which was reviewed favorably in *Time* (Feb. 27, 1978), is an adaptation of APA format using the less preferred, but valid number reference system [e.g., "Smith (3)" where (3) refers to the work's position in the reference list].

A Handbook for Scholars is largely valid criticism of scholarly writing that tends to be all too pedantic and obtuse. Van Leunen's aim is towards applying the studied simplicity of Strunk and White to academic works. Although much longer than *The Elements of Style, A Handbook for Scholars* addresses the researcher and academic writer explicitly and deals with issues pertinent to this breed. The book is highly readable, pointedly humorous, and very informative. It not only mirrors and amplifies the foibles of scholarly writers, but also shows how to improve written images.

In a separate article, van Leunen (1978b) also discusses the "singular notion," the pseudoscholarly avoidance of the first person. She attacks the way authors contort their words to avoid the first person. As such, the use of the passive voice, plural pronouns, and substitution of opinion for fact are rightfully satirized.

Words into Type

Skillin and Gay's (1974) *Words into Type* is another large, information-rich text. Although *Words into Type* also prescribes a style format, it is not included in the previous style manuals section for two reasons. First, the authors of this text have never seen a journal referring its writers to Skillin and Gay for style. Second, the focus of the manuscript style section of *Words into Type* is on the physical form of the manuscript (i.e., placement of block quotations, spacing between notes, type size and line spacing, form and content of tables, use of halftones and illustrations, and the like).

Words into Type offers more extensive information than even Chicago for working on copies and proofs for the publisher, preparing indices, and copy editing. Skillin and Gay also provide a great deal of information on punctuation and grammar. Two unique sections are included: composition in foreign languages and alphabets (largely derived from the 1973 U.S. Government Printing Office Style Manual) and the use and misuse of English words. Other sections include: five pages of trite expressions to be avoided; 23 pages of frequently misused and abused words with descriptions of their proper use, definitions, and sample uses; 15 pages of words with the preposition with which they are properly used; and a list of frequently encountered foreign phrases.

Other Writing Guides

Bernstein's (1971) beautifully titled *Miss Thistlebottom's Hobgoblins* is a volume dealing with what is subtitled "The Careful Writer's Guide to the Taboos, Bugbears, and Outmoded Rules of English Usage." He reviews words that are of questionable current use, syntactical aberrations of the language, too freely and unconsciously used idioms, and style of content in light, but caring, form.

A witty, cynical defense of the language is presented by the television and radio newsman Edwin Newman (1974) in his *Strictly Speaking: Will America Be the Death of English?* In narrative form, Newman takes issue with the barbarisms and vulgarisms all too common in written and spoken English. Newman takes aim primarily at the mass media, chiding them for setting linguistically improper standards for the general audience. His humor points out and, albeit a little obtusely, remedies the media-effected ills of American English.

The Writer's Manual (Cassidy, 1979) is a collection of essays on how to write for a variety of audiences. "The Mechanics of Writing and Getting Published" and "How to Write for Academic Publication" are two particularly informative chapters.

If more help of this nature is necessary, there are many different writing guides on the market that cannot be reviewed here. The

MLA Handbook provides a list of guides to writing and handbooks of composition. Campbell and Ballou (1974) provide a list with 25 entries including both style manuals and writing guides. There are also at least two journals directed toward the writer and the craft of writing: *The Writer* and *Writer's Digest.*

Lastly, there are two resources each writer should have close at hand: a good dictionary and a good thesaurus. "Good" denotes completeness and recency, particularly since the language does change over time. Meanings change in the same way knowledge changes. Resources should reflect the time in which the writer is working. A dictionary is a necessary resource for accuracy of spelling, meaning, word selection, and syllabication. A thesaurus can aid in selecting words most closely fitting the author's meaning (s) . As always, the goal is clear communication of what the author has to say. These resources are necessary for that end.

GUIDELINES FOR MANUSCRIPT SUBMISSION

APA, Chicago, MLA, and Skillin and Gay offer essentially the same guidelines for preparing a manuscript for submission for publication. The importance of this step is well described in the following quotation from the Chicago *Manual of Style*:

> The physical appearance of a manuscript is of immense importance to the whole publishing process. A well-prepared manuscript is very likely to influence the publisher's readers in its favor. Later, when accepted for publication, a tidy manuscript facilitates the work of the editor, the designer, the cost estimator, the typesetter, and the proofreader. Badly prepared copy makes for delays at every step . . . to say nothing of frayed nerves all around (p. 29)

A neat, well-prepared manuscript makes the entire publication process simpler and more efficient. An improperly or inconsistently prepared manuscript can lead to confusion and misinterpretation of content. Such errors can adversely affect the two main objectives —communication and publication.

Perhaps the one rule for manuscript preparation that is of prime importance is the necessity to double-space. This rule applies to text, illustrative matter, references, footnotes, index, and so on. It is the rare editor who will leave a manuscript untouched and the rare author who will see no need for corrections and comments. A single-spaced manuscript is difficult to read; changes on the paper will further affect legibility. For the same reasons, ample margins are necessary. APA indicates 1–1½ inches on all sides of the typed page is proper. This represents a 60 character pica type or a 72 character elite type line. It goes without saying that only one side of a sheet should be used. One type of paper should be used throughout the manuscript. This should be a medium- to heavy-weight bond paper; do not use erasable paper.

Errors in manuscript preparation are inevitable. Corrections should be made with correction paper or fluid. Strike overs are not acceptable; they can easily be misread. After the manuscript is completed and proofread closely for both mechanical and content errors, large scale errors or changes should be made by cutting out the passage to be discarded and pasting in the correct copy. The insert should be prepared in the same typeface as the rest of the manuscript. Briefer changes may be written or typed directly above the line to be amended or replaced. Passages to be replaced should be crossed out with a single, firm line.

All sections of the manuscript should begin on new pages and be numbered consecutively. Consecutive numbering will simplify estimating manuscript length in print. Text, tabular material, captions for figures, notes, references, and the like should be kept separate. Footnotes, especially, should be typed on separate pages because they will be set in a different typeface from the text at a different time.

APA gives strict guidelines regarding figures and tabular material. A separate page or section titled "Figure Captions" should contain all figure numbers and captions. Locations of figures, tables, and illustrations should be marked in the manuscript as a guide for the editor and typesetter. This should take the form of a clear instruction set off by lines above and below as in the following example:

Insert Table 10 about here

In this way, ample space will be left when figuring manuscript length.

When submitting the manuscript, do not staple or bind the pages. This will facilitate the editorial and typesetting process. At least two copies of the manuscript should be submitted. One copy should be the original, typed copy. The other (s) may be machine copies, if they are neat and legible (e.g., Xerox, mimeograph). Carbon copies are not acceptable.

Lastly, retain a copy of the manuscript. The postal service is not infallible nor are publishers. Retaining a copy of the final manuscript will make replacement simpler if it should be lost. Additionally, if photographs are included in the manuscript, have duplicates available. Photocopies of photographs cannot be used; glossy prints are necessary.

Table 6 presents a summary of the guidelines discussed above.

TABLE 6:   Guidelines for Manuscript Submission

---

1. Type, preferably with pica typeface.
2. Double-space, one side only.
3. Leave ample (1-1½ inch) margins on all four sides of the text.
4. Begin all sections—chapters, figures, notes, index, and so forth—on new pages.
5. Note locations for illustrative and tabular material in their appropriate place within the text.
6. Do not type numbers and captions of illustrative material on the figures. Prepare a separate page(s) titled "Figure Captions."
7. Number all pages consecutively.
8. Proofread for both mechanical and content errors.
9. Make corrections with correction paper or fluid. Do not strike-over errors. Cut and paste longer changes; type the new sections with the same type face as the rest of the manuscript.
10. Clip pages together; do not staple or bind.
11. Submit at least two copies of the manuscript. One should be the original ribbon copy. Other(s) may be machine copied. Do not submit carbon copies.
12. Retain a copy of the manuscript. Photographs retained should not be machine copies. Have duplicate prints made.

Note: The guidelines above have been abstracted from APA, Chicago, MLA, and Skillin & Gay.

7
COPYRIGHT
INFORMATION

Copyright is the protection of a work and of the temporal and monetary investment in its development. Laws regarding copyright are designed to protect not only the creator of work (producer's incentive), but also society and its interest in free expression and sharing of ideas (users' access). Copyright protection serves to attract the private and personal investments necessary to support creative expression. Property is the inducement offered in the form of rights in the expression created (Kurlantzick, 1978).

A new federal statute replaces the oft-amended Copyright Act of March 3, 1909, in determining who may hold copyright, what constitutes a copyrightable work, and what the limits of copyright are. The use of others' works in classroom teaching or educational writing requires adherence to the provisions of the Copyright Act of 1976, which went into effect on January 1, 1978. Beyond the limits of "fair use" (defined below), permission must be obtained and, if required, payment made for use of the work.

An author has the right to expect such protections for his or her own work. Yet the publish or perish atmosphere of the academic marketplace is not conducive to automatic compliance with these expectations. As both a creator and consumer of such works, the educational writer should be aware of the applicable provisions of copyright law.

COPYRIGHT LAW BEFORE 1976

Prior to the 1976 Act there existed two types of copyright protection: common law and statutory. Common law copyright protected all unpublished works from inception until publication (Budahl, 1971). Statutory copyright generally protected works once they were published. Confusions and difficulties resulted from this dual system. Further, technological developments in photocopying and other information duplication systems were not clearly treatable by application of the old law, even with amendments. The new Act arose from these pressures to deal comprehensively with copyright in a technological age.

THE 1976 COPYRIGHT STATUTE

The Copyright Act of 1976 (P.L. 94-553) eliminated the former dual system by providing federal statutory protection from the moment of creation of a work without regard to when or whether it is published. As Ringer (1976) pointed out, "creation (something the author does) thus supersedes publication (something the publisher does) as the pivotal copyright action" (p. 39). This protection applies to photocopying, offset reproduction, and other means of duplication and use.

The Act is the result of over half a century of case law and debate. The bill had been debated in the Congress since 1967 (Litz and Sparkman, 1977). The delays and revisions reflect changes in information technology (e.g., cable and closed circuit television) and in judicial interpretation (Zirkel, 1976).

Ownership of Copyright

The Copyright Act of 1976 affords copyright protection from

the date of creation of a work. The statute states explicitly that copyright belongs to a work's author (s) , except where works were created for hire or ownership was transferred to another, such as the publisher. Ownership of copyright and possession of the material object or work are different entities according to the Act. Transfer or change in possession of the material object does not cause transfer of copyright without some agreement to that effect (17 U.S.C. §202) .

In the case of works created for hire, unless there has been a written agreement otherwise, the employer is considered the author, and publication of the work must bear a copyright notice naming the employer as owner. The 1976 Act defines "works for hire" as existing only if the work is prepared as part of the author's official or *de facto* employment, or if the work is specially ordered or commissioned by another. More precisely, with respect to a commissioned work, the work will be considered for hire if it fits within one of the specific categories of commissioned works listed in the Act (17 U.S.C. §101) and if the parties expressly agree in writing that the work is for hire. Both conditions must be met.

No matter what the initial distribution of copyright ownership, it may be altered by contractual agreement (Kurlantzick, 1978) . Transfer of copyright ownership to journal publishers is frequently a requirement for publication. However, in the absence of an express transfer of the copyright, the Act states that "the owner of copyright in the collective work is presumed to have acquired only the privilege of reproducing and distributing the contribution as part of that particular collective work. . . ." (17 U.S.C. §201) . Should there be such a transfer, all fees and payments for use of a work or its parts belong to the publisher. Journals will typically outline their copyright policies in a statement to authors. Some of the "shopping guides" discussed in Chapter III indicate these journal copyright policies.

Notice and Registration of Copyright

The 1976 Act requires that a notice of copyright (the word "copyright," or a ©, the year of first publication, and the copyright owner's name) appear on the published copies of copyrighted works. The notice should be positioned "in such a manner

and location as to give reasonable notice of the claim of copyright"
(17 U.S.C. §401). Publication is defined as:

> [T]he distribution of copies or phono records of a work to the
> public by sale or other transfer of ownership, or by rental, lease,
> or lending. The offering to distribute copies or phono records to
> a group of persons for purposes of further distribution, public
> performance, or public display [also] constitutes publication. . . .
> (17 U.S.C. §101)

Under the 1909 Act, failure to place the copyright notice on a
published work led to loss of copyright protection, but under the
new Act lack of notice no longer automatically invalidates the
copyright. This fail-safe policy applies if an author's distribution
of her or his work is limited to a small number of copies or if registration with the Copyright Office is made within five years and
an effort is made to place a notice on future distributions (Ringer,
1976).

Registration of copyright is accomplished by submitting an application for copyright with the Register of Copyrights. Application forms may be obtained from the Register of Copyrights,
Library of Congress, Washington, D.C. 20559. A facsimile of the
front of the application form appears as Figure 5. Two copies of
the work and a fee (currently ten dollars) must accompany the
application. Deposit of the work and registration are treated as
separate, but related, requirements. Deposit of the work in the
Library of Congress must occur within three months of publication. Failure to make such a deposit or to respond to the Register
of Copyright's demands for deposit may result in fines but will not
invalidate the copyright (United States Copyright Office, 1977).
Guidelines for registration of copyright are prepared by the Copyright Office and may be obtained from the Register of Copyrights
at the above address.

Duration of Copyright

Under the 1976 Act, works created after January 1, 1978, have
a copyright term of the author's lifetime (or in the case of multiple authorship, the last surviving author's lifetime) plus an addi-

tional 50 years. Works made for hire, anonymous, and pseudonymous works have a term of 75 years from publication or 100 years from creation, whichever is shorter (17 U.S.C. §302). At the end of the term of copyright, the works revert to the public domain. Works that were in existence, but had not been published or registered or reverted to the public domain on January 1, 1978, have terms of copyright similar to those of new works. The life-plus 50 and 75/100 year-terms are equally applicable to such works with the provision that there be a minimum of 25 years of statutory protection and that the copyright not expire before December 31, 2002 (United States Copyright Office, 1978).

Under the 1909 Act, the duration of copyright was limited to two terms of 28 years each. The 1976 Act increases the second term to 47 years for a total of 75 years for works protected under the old Act as of January 1, 1978 (17 U.S.C. §304). Thus, those copyrights that had been renewed under the old Act and had not reached their 56-year expiration have had their terms extended to the full 75 years. Failure to renew copyright registration at the end of the first term of copyright results in expiration of the copyright (United States Copyright Office, 1978).

In all cases terms of copyright and deadlines for renewal extend to the end of the calendar year of expiration. Works presently in the public domain, works for which copyright protection has been lost, for whatever reason, and works whose terms of copyright have expired cannot be further copyrighted (Ringer, 1976).

Scope of Copyright

The Copyright Act of 1976 affords "exclusive rights to do and to authorize any of the following:

1. to reproduce the copyrighted work in copies or phonorecords;
2. to prepare derivative works based upon the copyrighted work;
3. to distribute copies or phonorecords . . . to the public by sale or other transfer of ownership, or by rental, lease, or lending;
4. in the case of literary . . . and other audiovisual works, to perform the copyrighted work publicly; and
5. in the case of literary . . . or other audiovisual works, to display the copyrighted works publicly." (17 U.S.C. §106)

FIGURE 5: **Facsimile of the Copyright Application Form**

FORM TX

UNITED STATES COPYRIGHT OFFICE

REGISTRATION NUMBER

TX   TXU

EFFECTIVE DATE OF REGISTRATION

....
Month   Day   Year

DO NOT WRITE ABOVE THIS LINE. IF YOU NEED MORE SPACE, USE CONTINUATION SHEET

(1) Title

TITLE OF THIS WORK: **PREVIOUS OR ALTERNATIVE TITLES:**

If a periodical or serial give: Vol. ...... No. ...... Issue Date ....

PUBLICATION AS A CONTRIBUTION: (If this work was published as a contribution to a periodical, serial, or collection, give information about the collective work in which the contribution appeared.)

Title of Collective Work: .... Vol. ...... No. ...... Date .... Pages ....

(2) Author(s)

IMPORTANT: Under the law, the "author" of a "work made for hire" is generally the employer, not the employee (see instructions). If any part of this work was "made for hire" check "Yes" in the space provided, give the employer (or other person for whom the work was prepared) as "Author" of that part, and leave the space for dates blank.

NAME OF AUTHOR: **DATES OF BIRTH AND DEATH:**

Born ...... Died ......
    (Year)   (Year)

1

Was this author's contribution to the work a "work made for hire"?   Yes...... No......

WAS THIS AUTHOR'S CONTRIBUTION TO THE WORK:

Anonymous?   Yes ......   No ......
Pseudonymous?   Yes ......   No ......

AUTHOR'S NATIONALITY OR DOMICILE:

Citizen of ....   or   {   Domiciled in ....
(Name of Country)   (Name of Country)

AUTHOR OF: (Briefly describe nature of this author's contribution)

If the answer to either of these questions is "Yes," see detailed instructions attached.

NAME OF AUTHOR:

Was this author's contribution to the work a "work made for hire"? Yes...... No......

2

AUTHOR'S NATIONALITY OR DOMICILE:

Citizen of .... } or { Domiciled in ....
(Name of Country)   (Name of Country)

AUTHOR OF: (Briefly describe nature of this author's contribution)

DATES OF BIRTH AND DEATH:

Born .... Died ....
(Year)   (Year)

WAS THIS AUTHOR'S CONTRIBUTION TO THE WORK:

Anonymous? Yes...... No......
Pseudonymous? Yes...... No......

If the answer to either of these questions is "Yes," see detailed instructions attached.

NAME OF AUTHOR:

Was this author's contribution to the work a "work made for hire"? Yes...... No......

3

AUTHOR'S NATIONALITY OR DOMICILE:

Citizen of .... } or { Domiciled in ....
(Name of Country)   (Name of Country)

AUTHOR OF: (Briefly describe nature of this author's contribution)

DATES OF BIRTH AND DEATH:

Born .... Died ....
(Year)   (Year)

WAS THIS AUTHOR'S CONTRIBUTION TO THE WORK:

Anonymous? Yes...... No......
Pseudonymous? Yes...... No......

If the answer to either of these questions is "Yes," see detailed instructions attached.

(3) Creation and Publication

YEAR IN WHICH CREATION OF THIS WORK WAS COMPLETED:

Year............

(This information must be given in all cases.)

DATE AND NATION OF FIRST PUBLICATION:

Date............
(Month)   (Day)   (Year)

Nation............
(Name of Country)

(Complete this block ONLY if this work has been published.)

(4) Claimant(s)

NAME(S) AND ADDRESS(ES) OF COPYRIGHT CLAIMANT(S):

TRANSFER: (If the copyright claimant(s) named here in space 4 are different from the author(s) named in space 2, give a brief statement of how the claimant(s) obtained ownership of the copyright.)

DO NOT WRITE HERE

Page 1 of .... pages

• Complete all applicable spaces (numbers 5-11) on the reverse side of this page
• Follow detailed instructions attached
• Sign the form at line 10

Penalties for copyright infringement range from $250 to $10,000. Courts may impose lesser ($100) or greater ($50,000) fines depending upon whether the infringement is innocent or willful (17 U.S.C. §504). The burden of proof in each situation is on the infringer (United States Copyright Office, 1977). The copyright holder also has the option of suing the infringer for actual damages and any additional profits. There is a three-year statute of limitations for both criminal and civil actions under the Act (17 U.S.C. §507).

Limitations of Copyright

The judgement doctrine of "fair use" allows copyrighted works to be reproduced without permission from or payment to the copyright owner when "the use is reasonable and not harmful to the rights of the copyright owner" (United States Copyright Office, 1977, p. A1:5). Although fair use is a flexible concept, "courts have consistently disallowed unauthorized educational uses—and their corresponding list of education 'excuses'—where their economic effects were evident" (Zirkel, 1976, p. 344). In determining whether a particular use is a fair use, the factors considered by courts and documented in the Act include:

- the purpose and character of the use, including whether such use is of a commercial nature or is for non-profit educational purposes;
- the nature of the copyrighted work;
- the amount and substantiality of the portion used in relation to the copyrighted work as a whole; and
- the effect of the use upon the potential market for or value of the copyrighted work. (17 U.S.C. §107)

Innocent intent is not considered an adequate defense in cases involving violation of fair use (Zirkel, 1976).

GUIDELINES FOR EDUCATIONAL USE

To more clearly define fair use with respect to classroom copying, a set of guidelines was drawn up by an ad hoc committee of representatives from over 40 groups of educational organizations, authors, users, and publishers (Magarell, 1978). These guidelines were incorporated in the report of the House of Representatives Judiciary Committee relative to the Act (United States House of Representatives, 1976; United States Copyright Office, 1978). A copy of these guidelines is presented in Appendix E. Roughly, these guidelines indicate that: (1) single copies may be made of a book chapter, article, short work, or illustration for the purpose of research or preparation for teaching; (2) multiple copies of short works (no more than one per student) may be made for classroom use provided that a notice of copyright is included on each copy.

Although the ad hoc committee had broad representation, neither the American Association of University Professors nor the Association of American Law Schools endorsed the guidelines. Both groups deemed that the guidelines, particularly the provisions regarding multiple copying, were too restrictive on the university level of classroom use (House of Representatives, 1976).

SOURCES OF FURTHER INFORMATION

Educational authors, as both creators and users of written works, need to be aware of copyright laws. Many writers may well need further information. Caughran's (1973) survey revealed a general lack of accurate knowledge among the teacher respondents concerning the limits of fair use and the penalties for copyright infringement.

The authoritative and comprehensive legal treatise is *Nimmer on Copyright* (1972). Several law review articles (e.g., Bloom, 1973; Cardozo, 1976, 1977; Zirkel, 1976) provide legal commentary about the copyright law as it applies to educators. There were many similar articles in educational journals before (e.g., Budahl, 1971; Heilprin, 1967; Wigren, 1968) and after (e.g., Balentine, 1977; Litz & Sparkman, 1977; Taubman, 1977) passage of the 1976 Copyright Act. Recent related resources directed specifically to educators are Miller's *Copyright and the Teaching/Learning Process* (1977) and *The New Copyright Law and Education* (1977).

Appendix A

AMERICAN EDUCATIONAL RESEARCH ASSOCIATION

1980 Annual Meeting
Call for Proposals

Boston
April 7-11

Ernst Z. Rothkopf, Chair
Program Committee

The 1980 Annual Meeting Program will emphasize the following thematic questions through invited events, but proposals relevant to them are especially encouraged.

- What accomplishments can be documented as research contributions to educational practice and the welfare of our society?

- What are appropriate standards for disciplined and creative inquiry into complex educational problems?

I General Information

The 1980 AERA Annual Meeting will be held April 7-11 in Boston. Proposals for papers, symposia, and other formal presentations will be considered for inclusion in the program if they are received by **August 15, 1979.**

The program will consist primarily of papers and symposia selected or invited by the Divisional Program Chairpersons. Special Interest Groups and the Association. In addition, there will be invited speakers, state-of-the-art presentations, graduate student programs, informal conversation hours and training events. All proposals submitted in response to this Call will be reviewed by at least two persons.

One and one-half hour time periods will be used throughout the meeting. Symposia requiring two hours will be scheduled either during the first period of the day to commence a half-hour earlier than the first session, or during the last period of the day to run a half-hour later than the last session.

All persons attending the meeting, including participants, are required to register. All sessions listed in the Program are open to anyone registered for the meeting. (Enrollment in training events is limited and fees are charged.)

Abstracts of presentations will be published in advance of the meeting. The Program will be mailed in February 1980, to all AERA members and to all nonmembers who register in advance for the meeting.

II General Regulations for Participation

- Any AERA member may submit a proposal for consideration.

- Any nonmember may submit a proposal if (a) an AERA member is a co-author of the paper, or if (b) an AERA member is a participant in the symposium being organized, or if (c) the proposer is sponsored by an active AERA member. An invitation from a member of the Program Committee to submit a proposal constitutes adequate sponsorship.

- A proposal may be submitted to *only one* division or Special Interest Group.

- An individual may appear on the program in not more than a total of four sessions, not to include participation as an invited speaker or in any session connected with an AERA office, e.g., business meetings, vice presidential addresses, or awards night.

- AERA does not pay for audio-visual equipment used by presenters. However, if the author indicates a need for A-V on the cover sheet submitted with the proposal, AERA will arrange for the equipment, coordinate the A-V scheduling, and prorate the costs among all A-V users. AERA will neither set up nor operate equipment. A-V rental facilities will be available locally for individual arrangements by persons who have not made prior arrangements through AERA. If A-V is essential to your presentation, so indicate on the cover sheet. The person signing the cover sheet will be invoiced for the equipment.

Inquiries relating to specific divisional or Special Interest Group areas of interest should be directed to the respective chairpersons (see Section V). General inquiries and requests for additional copies of the Call may be addressed to: AERA Meeting Coordinator, 1230 17th St., N.W., Washington, D.C. 20036.

III How to Submit Paper Proposals

A. General Information Concerning Paper Proposals

Authors are requested to include on the cover sheet descriptors for the subject index of the Program. These descriptors should be drawn or condensed from terms used in the descriptions in Section V of topic areas considered by each division.

- Modes of presentation for papers will consist of the following: (1) Small Roundtable sessions are group discussions with an individual author: (2) Poster sessions are individual presentations which must utilize display of graphic material and informal discussion: (3) Paper sessions are summary presentations of several individual papers with audience discussion immediately following each presentation; (4) Critique sessions are summary presentations of several papers followed by a prepared critique and audience discussion: (5) Single Presentation sessions consist of one individual presentation followed by one or more prepared critiques.

Decisions on the assignment of papers to a particular mode and the grouping of papers lie with the program chair. If any session format is unacceptable to the author, this should be indicated on the proposal.

- Session formats are not necessarily limited to the above. Innovative formats can be considered. If you wish to propose an innovative format, submit a description of the format in addition to the other materials required with the proposal to the appropriate division. Multimedia presentations are encouraged.

- **Authors assigned to a session involving a prepared discussion or critique are required to send the complete text of the paper to the discussants or critics by March 7, 1980. The session chairperson is authorized to drop from the program any author who does not do so.**

many of the following as are applicable, preferably in the order stated:

(a) Objectives
(b) Perspective(s) or theoretical framework
(c) Methods and/or techniques
(d) Data source
(e) Results and or conclusions
(f) Educational or scientific importance of the study.

The heading of the 2- to 3-page summary should use the following format:

In the upper left corner:
Title of Paper (caps and lower case)
Author(s) (all caps). Institution(s) (caps and lower case)

In the upper right corner:
Name of Presenting Author
Mailing Address

- **One-hundred-word Abstract** (for publication). Five copies. The abstract should be based on the outline given above for the summary. The abstract should conform as nearly as possible to standard English usage: *absolutely NO tabular or graphic material may be included*. It should be typed double-spaced on 8½" x 11" paper, and *carefully proofread*. An abstract which is longer than 100 words will be condensed or returned to the author for editing: such abstracts cannot be guaranteed publication. The heading of the abstract should be typed flush to the left margin, double-spaced, in the form below:

Title of Paper (caps and lower case)
Author(s) (all caps). Institution(s) (caps and lower case)

- **Envelopes.** Two self-addressed, stamped, business size envelopes for (a) acknowledgement of receipt of proposal and (b) notification of the decision of the Program Committee.

- **Index Cards.** Three 3" x 5" index cards, typed in the following format:

Name of Presenting Author (last name first)
Complete Mailing Address (with ZIP code)
Telephone Number (with area code)
Title of Presentation

IV How to Submit Symposium Proposals

A. General Information Concerning Symposium Proposals

• **Symposium.** A symposium is intended to provide an opportunity for the examination of specific problems or topics from a *variety of perspectives*. In addition to allowing for informative discussion, a symposium should provide for the presentation of alternative solutions or interpretations either of a common problem or in relation to a complementary theme. This purpose is best served when individuals with diverse or conflicting views are allowed to interact on a topic of sufficient scope and importance. It should be noted that a symposium should not be merely a presentation of a set of related papers. While such complementary papers are clearly worthwhile, they should be submitted as individual papers with an indication of suggested grouping on the cover sheet (see line 5 of the cover sheet).

• **Responsibilities of Organizers of Symposia.** It is the responsibility of organizers to suggest topics, solicit speakers, and suggest discussants. Organizers of symposia must have the consent of all participants *before* submitting the proposal. Organizers not wishing to chair the session must invite chairpersons. A presenter cannot also serve as chair. The organizer of a symposium is responsible for ascertaining that each person named as a participant will be present at the meeting if the session is accepted. Should unforeseen circumstances prevent a participant from attending, it is the responsibility of the organizer to find a suitable replacement and to notify the appropriate divisional chairperson. AERA central office and all other participants in the session. In addition, it is usually helpful for the participants and discussants involved in the session to have prior access to abstracts of each presentation so that they may formulate their remarks in the context of what the others plan to say. Organizers are urged to encourage such an exchange of information.

Only the organizer will be notified of the acceptance of a symposium, and in turn is responsible for notifying other participants in the symposium.

• Only papers which have not been previously published or presented at another professional meeting are eligible.

• It is the responsibility of the person whose name appears as the presenting author of an accepted proposal to appear at the Annual Meeting to present the paper. If unforeseen circumstances arise which prevent him or her from presenting the paper, it is the author's responsibility to arrange for someone else to make the presentation and send notice of the replacement to the AERA central office, the program chairperson of the sponsoring division or SIG, and the chairperson of the session.

• Even though a complete paper will not be read in any of the presentation modes used at the meeting, a complete paper must be available. In advance of the meeting, each author, except those in Small Roundtables and Poster sessions, must send a copy of the presentation to the chairperson, critic and/or discussants in the session. Authors in Small Roundtables and Poster sessions are encouraged to bring copies of papers or materials to the session.

• AERA reserves the right to publish or otherwise reproduce and distribute summaries of all accepted papers. Unless expressly prohibited in writing by the author, the summaries will also be made available to the press on request. Such dissemination does not preclude subsequent publication of the summary or the complete paper by the author.

B. Materials to be Submitted with a Paper Proposal

• **Paper Proposal Cover Sheet.** (With this Call — p. C-7) Five copies. with all items, including subject descriptors, completed.

• **Summary.** Five copies of a 2- to 3-page (8½" x 11" paper) single-spaced summary, for use in judging the merits of the proposed paper. A summary exceeding this limit may cause a paper to be refused without review. The summary should explicitly deal with as

---

Appendix B

ERIC CLEARINGHOUSES

ERIC Clearinghouse on *Adult, Career, and Vocational Education*
Ohio State University
National Center for Research in Vocational Education
1960 Kenny Road
Columbus, Ohio 43210
Telephone: (614) 486-3655

Adult, career, and vocational education, formal and informal at all levels, encompassing attitudes, self-knowledge, and specific vocational and occupational skills; adult and continuing education, formal and informal, relating to occupational, family, leisure, citizen, organizational, and retirement roles; vocational and technical education, including new sub-professional fields, industrial arts, and vocational rehabilitation for the handicapped.

ERIC Clearinghouse on *Handicapped and Gifted Children*
Council for Exceptional Children
1920 Association Drive
Reston, Virginia 22091
Telephone: (703) 620-3660

Aurally handicapped, visually handicapped, mentally handicapped, developmentally disabled, abused/neglected, autistic, multiply handicapped, severely handicapped, physically handicapped, emotionally disturbed, speech handicapped, learning disabled, and the gifted and the talented; behavioral, psychomotor, and communication disorders, administration of special education services; preparation and continuing education of professional and paraprofessional personnel; preschool learning and development of the exceptional; general studies on creativity.

ERIC Clearinghouse on *Counseling and Personnel Services*
University of Michigan
School of Education Building, Room 2108
Ann Arbor, Michigan 48109
Telephone: (313) 764-9492

Preparation, practice, and supervision of counselors at all educational levels and in all settings; theoretical development of counseling and guidance; use and results of personnel procedures such as testing, interviewing, disseminating, and analyzing such information; group work and case work; nature of pupil, student, and adult characteristics; personnel workers and their relation to career planning, family consultations, and student orientation activities.

ERIC Clearinghouse on *Educational Management*
University of Oregon
Eugene, Oregon 97403
Telephone: (503) 686-5043

Leadership, management, and structure of public and private educational organizations; practice and theory of administration; preservice and inservice preparation of administrators, tasks, and processes of administration; methods and varieties of organization, organizational change, and social context of the organization. Sites, buildings, and equipment for education; planning, financing, constructing, renovating, equipping, maintaining, operating, insuring, utilizing, and evaluating educational facilities.

ERIC Clearinghouse on *Elementary & Early Childhood Education*
University of Illinois
College of Education
Urbana, Illinois 61801
Telephone: (217) 333-1386

Prenatal factors, parental behavior; the physical, psychological, social, educational, and cultural development of children from birth through the primary grades; educational theory, research, and practice related to the development of young children, including teacher preparation, educational programs and curricula related community services, groups and institutions, administration, and physical settings as well as theoretical and philosophical issues. Includes both the early years of childhood (ages 0-7) and the "middle years" (ages 8-12).

ERIC Clearinghouse on *Higher Education*
George Washington University
One Dupont Circle, N.W., Suite 630
Washington, D.C. 20036
Telephone: (202) 296-2597

Various subjects relating to college and university students, college and university conditions and problems, college and university programs. Curricular and instructional problems and programs, faculty, institutional research. Federal programs, professional education (medical, law, etc.), graduate education, university extension programs, teaching-learning, planning, governance, finance, evaluation, interinstitutional arrangements, and management of higher educational institutions.

ERIC Clearinghouse on *Information Resources*
Syracuse University
School of Education
130 Huntington Hall
Syracuse, New York 13210
Telephone: (315) 423-3640

Management, operation, and use of libraries; the technology to improve their operation and the education, training, and professional activities of librarians and information specialists. Educational techniques involved in microteaching, systems analysis, and programmed instruction employing audiovisual teaching aids and technology, such as television, radio, computers, and cable television, communication satellites, microforms, and public television.

ERIC Clearinghouse for *Junior Colleges*
University of California
Powell Library, Room 96
405 Hilgard Avenue
Los Angeles, California 90024
Telephone: (213) 825-3931

Development, administration, and evaluation of two-year public and private community and junior colleges. Junior college students, staff, curricula, programs, libraries, and community services.

ERIC Clearinghouse on *Languages and Linguistics*
Center for Applied Linguistics
1611 North Kent Street
Arlington, Virginia 22209
Telephone: (703) 528-4312

Languages and linguistics. Instructional methodology, psychology of language learning, cultural and intercultural content, application of linguistics; curricular problems and developments, teacher training and qualifications, language sciences, psycho-linguistics, theoretical and applied linguistics, language pedagogy, bilingualism, and commonly taught languages including English for speakers of other languages.

ERIC Clearinghouse on *Reading and Communication Skills*
National Council of Teachers of English
1111 Kenyon Road
Urbana, Illinois 61801
Telephone: (217) 328-3870

Reading, English, and communication skills (verbal and non-verbal), preschool through college. Educational research and development in reading, writing, speaking, and listening. Identification, diagnosis and remediation of reading problems. Speech communication — forensics, mass communication, interpersonal and small group interaction, interpretation, rhetorical and communication theory, instruction development, speech sciences, and theater. Preparation of instructional staff and related personnel in these areas.

All aspects of reading behavior with emphasis on physiology, psychology, sociology, and teaching. Instructional materials, curricula, tests and measurement, preparation of reading teachers and specialists, and methodology at all levels. Role of libraries and other agencies in fostering and guiding reading. Diagnostic and remedial services in school and clinical settings

ERIC Clearinghouse on *Teacher Education*
American Association of Colleges for Teacher Education
One Dupont Circle, N.W., Suite 616
Washington, D.C. 20036
Telephone: (202) 293-7280

School personnel at all levels; all issues from selection through preservice and inservice preparation and training to retirement; curricula; educational theory and philosophy; general education not specifically covered by the Educational Management Clearinghouse. All aspects of physical education.

ERIC Clearinghouse on *Tests, Measurement, and Evaluation*
Educational Testing Service
Rosedale Road
Princeton, New Jersey 08541
Telephone: (609) 921-9000 ext. 2176

Tests and other measurement devices; methodology of measurement and evaluation; application of tests, measurement, or evaluation in educational projects or programs.

ERIC Clearinghouse on *Urban Education*
Teachers College, Columbia University
Box 40
525 W. 120th Street
New York, New York 10027
Telephone: (212) 678-3437

ERIC Clearinghouse on *Rural Education and Small Schools*

New Mexico State University

Box 3 AP

Las Cruces, New Mexico 88003

Telephone: (505) 646-2623

Education of Indian Americans, Mexican Americans, Spanish Americans, and migratory farm workers and their children; outdoor education; economic, cultural, social, or other factors related to educational programs in rural areas and small schools.

ERIC Clearinghouse for *Science, Mathematics, and Environmental Education*

Ohio State University

1200 Chambers Road, Third Floor

Columbus, Ohio 43212

Telephone: (614) 422-6717

All levels of science, mathematics, and environmental education. Within these fields, development of curriculum and instructional materials; media applications; impact of interest, intelligence, values, and concept development upon learning; preservice and inservice teacher education and supervision.

ERIC Clearinghouse for *Social Studies/Social Science Education*

855 Broadway

Boulder, Colorado 80302

Telephone: (303) 492-8434

All levels of social studies and social science; content of disciplines; applications of learning theory, curriculum theory, child development theory, and instructional theory; research and development programs; special needs of student groups; education as a social science; history of education; comparative education; social studies/social science and the community; humanities education.

periences and environments from birth onward; the academic, intellectual, and social performance of urban children and youth in all schools from grade three through college entrance (including the effect of self concept, motivation, and other affective influences); education of urban, Puerto Rican and Asian American populations, and rural and urban black populations; programs and practices which provide learning experiences designed to meet the special needs of diverse populations served by urban schools and which build upon their unique as well as their common characteristics; structural changes in the classroom, school, school system, and community and innovative instructional practices which directly affect urban children and youth; programs, practices, and materials related to economic and ethnic discrimination, segregation, desegregation, and integration in education; issues, programs, practices, and materials related to redressing the curriculum imbalance in the treatment of ethnic minority groups.

Educational Resources Information Center

(Central ERIC)

National Institute of Education

Washington, D.C. 20208

Telephone: (202) 254-7934

ERIC Processing & Reference Facility

4833 Rugby Avenue, Suite 303

Bethesda, Maryland 20014

Telephone: (301) 656-9723

ERIC Document Reproduction Service

P.O. Box 190

Arlington, Virginia 22210

Telephone: (703) 841-1212

Oryx Press

3930 East Camelback Road, Suite 206

Phoenix, Arizona 85018

Telephone: (602) 956-6233

Appendix C

NEW JOURNALS IN EDUCATION

Journal Name and Address	*Focus*
Action in Teacher Education John F. Sikula, Editor Division of Education Indiana University Northwest Gary, IN 46400	Articles on concepts, practices, and research in teacher education, which have practical applications or implications for teaching (Thematic journal published by Association of Teacher Educators)
Contemporary Education & Psychology Allen J. Edwards, Editor Psychology Department Southwest Missouri State University Springfield, MO 65800	Empirical research and theoretical articles in educational psychology
Curriculum Inquiry Leonard Berk and Joel Weiss, Editors Ontario Institute for Studies in Education University of Toronto 252 Bloor Street W. Toronto, Ontario M5S IV6 CANADA	Articles from various disciplines in curriculum development and evaluation
Education & Treatment of Children (ETC) Robert F. Dickie and Daniel Hursch, Editors Pressley Ridge School 530 Marshall Avenue Pittsburgh, PA 15214	Articles for broad audiences of practitioners (including teachers, counselors, therapists, social workers)

Journal Name and Address	*Focus*
Education R&D Report Council for Educational Development & Research 1518 K Street N.W. Suite 206 Washington, D.C. 20006	Practitioner-oriented reporting of educational events and needs
Education Unlimited Barbara Aiello, Editor Educational Resources Center 1834 Meetinghouse Road Boothwyn, Pa. 19061	Practical articles relevant to improving educational experi- ences for special students in the least restrictive environments
Educational Evaluation and Policy Analysis W. James Popham, Editor American Educational Research Association 1230 17th Street N.W. Washington, D.C. 20036	Articles on educational evalua- tion, educational policy analy- sis, and the relationship be- tween the two activities
Educational Research Quarterly S.J. Knezevich, Editor School of Education WPH 1101 University of Southern California Los Angeles, CA 90007	Articles describing research studies and conceptual models
Evaluation and the Health Professions R. Parker Bausell and Carolyn Waltz, Editors Empirical Publications P.O. Box 13345 Baltimore, MD 21203	Empirical articles relating to health education and related fields
Executive Educator c/o The American School Board Journal 1055 Thomas Jefferson Street, N.W. Washington, D.C. 20007	Major articles providing time- ly, sophisticated, and inside in- formation to public school ad- ministrators
International Journal for Advancement of *Counseling* Nathan Deen, John Paterson, Douwe de Vires, Editors c/o Martinus Nijoff Publishers P.O. Box 442 The Hague, The Netherlands	Articles on counseling from various countries

Journal Name and Address	*Focus*
International Journal of Career and Continuing Education Phillip J. Sleeman, Executive Editor Center for Media and Technology, U-1 University of Connecticut Storrs, CT 06268	Descriptive and research-based articles covering school, industry, and community instructional and training programs
International Journal of Political Education Elsevier Scientific Publishing Company Jan van Galenstraat 335 P.O. Box 330 Amsterdam, The Netherlands	Comparative studies on socialization theory and research; articles on the development of political competence; reviews of curricula and programs of various countries
Journal of Comparative Cultures 9332 Vista Bonita Cypress, CA 90630	Articles on crosscultural studies and multicultural education
Journal of Development and Remedial Education Center for Developmental Education Appalachian State University Boone, NC 28607	Articles concerning the education of underprepared students at the post-secondary level
NABE Journal Jose Vasquez, Editor Hunter College 695 Park Avenue New York, NY	Articles on bilingual education
Perceptions Box 142 Millburn, NJ 07041	Newsletter articles on practical teaching methods parents can use at home to help educate their learning disabled children
Science Education N.E. Bingham, Editor	Research articles and position papers on science education
Journal of Research on Science Teaching David P. Butts, Editor John Wiley & Sons Wiley-Interscience Division 605 Third Avenue New York, NY 10016	

Journal Name and Address	*Focus*
Studies in Educational Evaluation Marvin Alkin, Associate Editor Center for the Study of Evaluation University of California at Los Angeles Los Angeles, CA	Empirical and nonempirical studies focusing on practical aspects of appraising instructional methods and materials from various disciplines and countries
Texas Tech Journal of Education Robert H. Anderson, Editor Texas University Lubbock, TX 79409	Research, theoretical, and practical articles

Appendix D

GUIDELINES FOR NONSEXIST LANGUAGE IN APA JOURNALS

The *Publication Manual* of the American Psychological Association (1974, p. 28) suggests that journal authors "be aware of the current move to avoid generic use of male nouns and pronouns when content refers to both sexes . . . [and] avoid overuse of the pronoun *he* when *she* or *they* is equally appropriate." The first change sheet to the *Publication Manual* (1975, p. 2) says: "For some specific suggestions on how to avoid such language, see 'Guidelines for Nonsexist Use of Language,' which was prepared by the APA Task Force on Issues of Sexual Bias in Graduate Education and published in the June 1975 *American Psychologist* (pp. 682–684)." Those guidelines, while helpful, are not specific to journal articles.

This second change sheet states the policy on sexist language in APA journals, offers some general principles for journal authors to consider, and suggests some ways to avoid sexist language.

To obtain single copies of this change sheet, send a stamped, self-addressed envelope to Publication Manual, Change Sheet 2, American Psychological Association, 1200 Seventeenth Street, N.W., Washington, D.C. 20036.

POLICY STATEMENT

APA as a publisher accepts journal authors' word choices unless those choices are inaccurate, unclear, or ungrammatical. However, because APA as an organization is committed to both science and the fair treatment of individuals and groups, authors of journal articles are expected to avoid writing in a manner that reinforces questionable attitudes and assumptions about people and sex roles.

Language that reinforces sexism can spring from subtle errors in research design, inaccurate interpretation, or imprecise word choices. Faulty logic in design, for example, may lead an investigator to report sex differences when the stimulus materials and measures used give one sex an unwarranted advantage over the other. Or, in interpretation, an investigator may make unwarranted generalizations about all people from data about one sex. Imprecise word choices, which occur frequently in journal writing, may be interpreted as biased, discriminatory, or demeaning even if they are not intended to be.

Advice on research design and interpretation is beyond the scope of the APA *Publication Manual*. However, in the spirit of the guidelines on writing style in Chapter 2, the following guidelines on nonsexist language are intended to help authors recognize and change instances where word choices may be inaccurate, misleading, or discriminatory.

Reprinted courtesy of the American Psychological Association.

GUIDELINES

Sexism in journal writing may be classified into two categories that are conceptually different: problems of *designation* and problems of *evaluation*.

Problems of Designation

An author must use care in choosing words to ensure accuracy, clarity, and freedom from bias. In the case of sexism, long-established cultural practice can exert a powerful insidious influence over even the most conscientious author. Nouns, pronouns, and adjectives that designate persons can be chosen to eliminate, or at least to minimize, the possibility of ambiguity in sex identity or sex role. In the following examples, problems of designation are divided into two subcategories: *ambiguity of referent,* where it is unclear whether the author means one or both sexes, and *stereotyping,* where the writing conveys unsupported or biased connotations about sex roles and identity.

Problems of Evaluation

By definition, scientific writing should be free of implied or irrelevant evaluation of the sexes. Difficulties may derive from the habitual use of clichés, or familiar expressions, such as "man and wife." The use of *man and wife* together implies differences in the freedom and activities of each, and evaluation of roles can occur. Thus, *husband and wife* are parallel, *man and wife* are not. In the examples that follow, problems of evaluation, like problems of designation, are divided into *ambiguity of referent* and *stereotyping.*

I. Problems of Designation

Examples of common usage	Consider meaning. An alternative may be better.	Comment

A. Ambiguity of Referent

Examples of common usage	Consider meaning. An alternative may be better.	Comment
1. The *client* is usually the best judge of the value of *his* counseling.	The *client* is usually the best judge of the value of counseling.	*His* deleted.
	Clients are usually the best judges of the value of the counseling they receive.	Changed to plural.
	The best judge of the value of counseling is usually *the client*.	Rephrased.
2. *Man's search* for knowledge has led *him* into ways of learning that bear examination.	*The search* for knowledge has led *us* into ways of learning that bear examination.	Rephrased, using first person.
	People have continually sought knowledge. The search has led them, etc. . . .	Rewritten in two sentences.
3. man, mankind	people, humanity, human beings, humankind, human species	In this group of examples, a variety of terms may be substituted.
man's achievements	human achievements, achievements of the human species	
the average man	the average person, people in general	

Examples of common usage	Consider meaning. An alternative may be better.	Comment
man a project	staff a project, hire personnel, employ staff	
manpower	work force, personnel, workers	
Department of Manpower	(No alternative.)	Official titles should not be changed.
4. The use of experiments in psychology presupposes the mechanistic nature of *man*.	The use of experiments in psychology presupposes the mechanistic nature of the *human being*.	Noun substituted.
5. This interference phenomenon, called learned helplessness, has been demonstrated in rats, cats, fish, dogs, monkeys, and *men*.	This intereference phenomenon, called learned helplessness, has been demonstrated in rats, cats, fish, dogs, monkeys, and *humans*.	Noun substituted.
6. Issues raised were whether the lack of cardiac responsivity in the premature *infant* is secondary to *his* heightened level of autonomic arousal . . .	. . . responsivity in the premature *infant* is secondary to *the* heightened level . . . . . . responsivity in premature *infants* is secondary to *their* heightened levels. . .	*His* changed to *the*. Rewritten in plural.
7. First the *individual* becomes aroused by violations of *his* personal space, and then *he* attrib-	First *we* become aroused by violations of *our* personal space, and then *we* attribute the cause of this	Pronouns substituted, *he* and *his* omitted.

Original	Revision	Comment
utes the cause of this arousal to other people in *his* environment.	arousal to other people in *the* environment.	
8. Much has been written about the effect that a *child's* position among *his* siblings has on *his* intellectual development.	Much has been written about the relationship between sibling position and intellectual development in *children*.	Rewritten, plural introduced.
9. Subjects were 16 girls and 16 boys. Each *child* was to place a car on *his* board so that two cars and boards looked alike.	Each child was to place a car on *his or her* board so that two cars and boards looked alike.	Changed *his* to *his or her*; however, use sparingly to avoid monotonous repetition. *Her or his* may also be used, but it sounds awkward. In either case, keep pronoun order consistent to avoid ambiguity.
10. Each person's alertness was measured by the difference between *his* obtained relaxation score and *his* obtained arousal score.	Each person's alertness was measured by the difference between *the* obtained relaxation and arousal scores.	*His* deleted, plural introduced.
11. The client's husband *lets* her teach part-time.	The client's husband *"lets"* her teach part-time. The husband says he *"lets"* the client teach part-time. The client *says her husband "lets"* her teach part-time.	Punctuation added to clarify location of the bias, that is, with husband and wife, not with author. If necessary, rewrite to clarify as allegation. See Example 24 below.

B. Stereotyping

Original	Revision	Comment
12. males, females	men, women, boys, girls, adults, children, adolescents	Specific nouns reduce possibility of stereotypic bias and often clarify dis-

Examples of common usage	Consider meaning. An alternative may be better.	Comment
		cussion. Use *male* and *female* as adjectives where appropriate and relevant (female experimenter, male subject). Avoid unparallel usages such as 10 *men* and 16 *females*.
13. Research scientists often neglect their *wives* and *children*.	Research scientists often neglect their *families*.	Alternative wording acknowledges that women as well as men are research scientists.
14. When a *test developer or test user* fails to satisfy these requirements, *he* should . . .	When *test developers or test users* fail to satisfy these requirements, *they* should . . .	Same as Example 13.
15. the psychologist . . . *he*	psychologists . . . *they*; the psychologist . . . *she*	Be specific or change to plural if discussing women as well as men.
the therapist . . . *he*	therapists . . . *they*; the therapist . . . *she*	
the nurse . . . *she*	nurses . . . *they*; nurse . . . *he*	
the teacher . . . *she*	teachers . . . *they*; teacher . . . *he*	
16. woman doctor, lady lawyer, male nurse	doctor, physician, lawyer, nurse	Specify sex if it is a variable or if sex designation is necessary to the discussion ("13 female doctors and 22 male doctors").

17. mothering	parenting, nurturing (or specify exact behavior)	Noun substituted.
18. chairman (of an academic department)	Use *chairperson* or *chair* if it is known that the institution has established either form as an official title. Otherwise use *chairman*.	*Department head* may be appropriate, but the term is not synonymous with *chairman* and *chairperson* at all institutions.
chairman (presiding officer of a committee or meeting)	chairperson, moderator, discussion leader	In parliamentary usage *chairman* is the official term. Alternatives are acceptable in most writing.
19. Only *freshmen* were eligible for the project.	(No alternative if academic standing is meant.)	*First-year student* is often an acceptable alternative to *freshman*, but in these cases, *freshmen* is used for accuracy.
All the students had matriculated for three years, but the majority were still *freshmen*.		
20. foreman, policeman, stewardess, mailman	supervisor, police officer, flight attendant, postal worker or letter carrier	Noun substituted.

II. Problems of Evaluation

A. Ambiguity of Referent

21. The authors acknowledge the assistance of *Mrs. John Smith.*	The authors acknowledge the assistance of *Jane Smith.*	Use given names in author acknowledgments. When forms of address are used in text, use the appropriate form: Mr., Mrs., Miss, or Ms.

Examples of common usage	Consider meaning. An alternative may be better.	Comment
22. men and women, sons and daughters, boys and girls, husbands and wives	women and men, daughters and sons, girls and boys, wives and husbands	Vary the order if content does not require traditional order.

B. Stereotyping

Examples of common usage	Consider meaning. An alternative may be better.	Comment
23. men and girls	men and women, women and men	Use parallel terms. Of course, use *men and girls* if that is literally what is meant.
24. The client's husband lets her teach part-time.	The client teaches part-time.	The author of this example intended to communicate the working status of the woman but inadvertently revealed a stereotype about husband-wife relationships; *see* Example 11 above.
25. ambitious men and aggressive women	ambitious women and men or ambitious people	Some adjectives, depending on whether the person described is a man or a woman, connote bias. The examples illustrate some common usages that may not always convey exact meaning, especially when paired, as in column 1.
	aggressive men and women or aggressive people	
cautious men and timid women	cautious women and men, cautious people	
	timid men and women or timid people	

26. The boys chose typically male toys.	The boys chose (specify)	Being specific reduces possibility of stereotypic bias.
The client's behavior was typically female.	The client's behavior was (specify)	
27. woman driver	driver	If specifying sex is necessary, use *female driver*.
28. The *girls* in the office greeted all clients.	secretaries, office assistants	Noun substituted.
29. coed	female student	Noun substituted.
30. women's lib, women's libber	women's movement, feminist, supporter of women's movement	Noun substituted.
31. Subjects were 16 men and 4 women. *The women were housewives.*	The men were (specify) and the women were (specify).	Dscribe women and men in parallel terms. *Housewife* indicates sex, marital status, and occupation, and excludes men. *Homemaker* indicates occupation, and includes men.

A FINAL WORD

Attempting to introduce nonsexist language at the cost of awkwardness, obscurity, or euphemistic phrasing does not improve scientific communication. An author should make clear that both sexes are under discussion when they are and should indicate sex when only one sex is discussed. Under no circumstances should an author hide sex identity in an attempt to be unbiased, if knowledge of sex may be important to the reader.

Any endeavor to change the language is an awesome task at best. Some aspects of our language that may be considered sexist are firmly embedded in our culture, and we presently have no acceptable substitutes. In English, the use of third-person singular pronouns is one example: the generic use of *he* is misleading, *it* is inaccurate, *one* conveys a different meaning, and *he or she* can become an annoying repetition. Nevertheless, with some rephrasing and careful attention to meaning, even the generic *he* can be avoided most of the time. The result of such efforts is accurate, unbiased communication, the purpose of these guidelines.

Suggested Reading

APA Task Force on Issues of Sexual Bias in Graduate Education. Guidelines for nonsexist use of language. *American Psychologist*, 1975, *30*, 682–684.

Burr, E., Dunn, S., & Farquhar, N. *Guidelines for equal treatment of the sexes in social studies textbooks*. Los Angeles: Westside Women's Committee, 1973. (Available from Westside Women's Committee, P.O. Box 24D20, Los Angeles, California 90024.)

DeBoard, D., Fisher, A. M., Moran, M. C., & Zawodny, L. *Guidelines to promote the awareness of human potential*. Philadelphia, Pa.: Lippincott, undated.

Harper & Row. *Harper & Row guidelines on equal treatment of the sexes in textbooks*. New York: Author, 1976.

Henley, N., & Thorne, B. *She said/he said: An annotated bibliography of sex differences in language, speech, and nonverbal communication*. Pittsburgh, Pa.: Know, 1975. (Available from Know, Inc., P.O. Box 86031, Pittsburgh, Pennsylvania 15221.)

Holt, Rinehart & Winston (College Department). *The treatment of sex roles and minorities*. New York: Author, 1976.

Lakoff, R. *Language and woman's place*. New York: Harper & Row, 1975.

Lerner, H. E. Girls, ladies, or women? The unconscious dynamics of language choice. *Comprehensive Psychiatry*, 1976, *17*, 295–299.

McGraw-Hill. *Guidelines for equal treatment of the sexes in McGraw-Hill*

Book Company publications. New York: Author, undated.

Miller, C., & Swift, K. *Words and women.* Garden City, N.Y.: Anchor Press/Doubleday, 1976.

Prentice-Hall. *Prentice-Hall author's guide* (5th ed.) . Englewood Cliffs, N.J.: Author, 1975.

Random House. *Guidelines for multiethnic/nonsexist survey.* New York: Author, 1975.

Scott, Foresman. *Guidelines for improving the image of women in textbooks.* Glenview, Ill.: Author, 1974.

John Wiley & Sons. *Wiley guidelines on sexism in language.* New York: Author, 1977.

This change sheet was prepared by the APA Publication Manual Task Force. Members of the task force are Charles N. Cofer (Chairperson) , Robert S. Daniel, Frances Y. Dunham, and Walter I. Heimer. Ellen Kimmel served as liaison from the Committee on Women in Psychology, and Anita DeVivo as APA staff liaison. This material may be reproduced in whole or in part without permission, provided that acknowledgment is made to the American Psychological Association.

Appendix E

"FAIR USE" GUIDELINES
FOR CLASSROOM COPYING

I. Single Copying for Teachers

A single copy may be made of any of the following by or for a teacher at his or her individual request for his or her scholarly research or use in teaching or preparation to teach a class:

A. A chapter from a book;

B. An article from a periodical or newspaper;

C. A short story, short essay or short poem, whether or not from a collective work;

D. A chart, graph, diagram, drawing, cartoon or picture from a book, periodical, or newspaper;

II. Multiple Copies for Classroom Use

Multiple copies (not to exceed in any event more than one copy per pupil in a course) may be made by or for the teacher

United States House of Representatives, H.R. 94-1476 (1976); United States Copyright Office (1978).

giving the course for classroom use or discussion; *provided that*:

A. The copying meets the tests of brevity and spontaneity as defined below; *and*,

B. Meets the cumulative effect test as defined below; *and*,

C. Each copy includes a notice of copyright

Definitions

> *Brevity*

(i) Poetry: (a) A complete poem if less than 250 words and if printed on not more than two pages or, (b) from a longer poem, an excerpt of not more than 250 words.

(ii) Prose: (a) Either a complete article, story or essay of less than 2,500 words, or (b) an excerpt from any prose work of not more than 1,000 words or 10% of the work, whichever is less, but in any event a minimum of 500 words.

[Each of the numerical limits stated in "i" and "ii" above may be expanded to permit the completion of an unfinished line of a poem or of an unfinished prose paragraph.]

(iii) Illustration: One chart, graph, diagram, drawing, cartoon or picture per book or per periodical issue.

(iv) "Special" works: Certain works in poetry, prose, or in "poetic prose" which often combine language with illustrations and which are intended sometimes for children and at other times for a more general audience fall short of 2,500 words in their entirety. Paragraph "ii" above notwithstanding such "special works" may not be reproduced in their entirety; however, an excerpt comprising not more than two of the published pages of such special work and containing not more than 10% of the words found in the text thereof, may be reproduced.

> *Spontaneity*

(i) The copying is at the instance and inspiration of the individual teacher, and

(ii) The inspiration and decision to use the work and

the moment of its use for maximum teaching effectiveness are so close in time that it would be unreasonable to expect a timely reply to a request for permission.

Cumulative Effect

(i) The copying of the material is for only one course in the school in which the copies are made.

(ii) Not more than one short poem, article, story, essay, or two excerpts may be copied from the same author, nor more than three from the same collective work or periodical volume during one class term.

(iii) There shall not be more than nine instances of such multiple copying for one course during one class term.

[The limitations stated in "ii" and "iii" above shall not apply to current news periodicals and newspapers and current news sections of other periodicals.]

III. Prohibitions as to I and II Above

Notwithstanding any of the above, the following shall be prohibited:

A. Copying shall not be used to create or to replace or substitute for anthologies, compilations, or collective works. Such replacement or substitution may occur whether copies of various works or excerpts therefrom are accumulated or reproduced and used separately.

B. There shall be no copying of or from works intended to be "consumable" in the course of study or of teaching. These include workbooks, exercises, standardized tests and test booklets and answer sheets, and like consumable material.

C. Copying shall not:

(a) substitute for the purchase of books, publishers' reprints, or periodicals;

(b) be directed by higher authority;

(c) be repeated with respect to the same item by the teacher from term to term.

D. No charge shall be made to the student beyond the actual cost of the photocopying.

References

American Mathematical Society. *A manual for authors of mathematical papers.* Providence, R.I.: Author, 1962.

American Psychological Association. *Publication manual* (2nd ed.). Washington, D.C.: Author, 1974.

American Psychological Association. *Cumulative author index to psychological abstracts.* Washington, D.C.: Author, 1975. (a)

American Psychological Association. *Cumulative subject index to psychological abstracts.* Washington, D.C.: Author, 1975. (b)

American Psychological Association. *Thesaurus of psychological index terms* (2nd ed.). Washington, D.C.: Author, 1977.

American Psychological Association. *Psychological abstracts.* Washington, D.C.: Author, 1978—.

APA Task Force on Issues of Sexual Bias in Graduate Education. Guidelines for non-sexist use of language. *American Psychologist,* 1975, *30,* 682–684.

111

Appelbaum, J., & Evans, N. *How to get happily published.* New York: Harper & Row, 1978.

Arnold, D.B., & Doyle, K.O., Jr. *Education/psychology journals: A scholar's guide.* Metuchen, N.J.: Scarecrow Press, 1975.

Associated Press Managing Editors Association. *The Associated Press stylebook.* Dayton, Ohio: Lorenz Press, 1977.

Ayer directory of publications. Philadelphia: Ayer Press, 1978.

Balentine, R.S. The new copyright law and the public schools. *School Law Bulletin,* 1977, *8* (1), 1–5.

Barber, V. How to negotiate a publishing contract. *Change,* 1975, *7* (3), 61–63.

Barcombe, W.A. On writing textbooks. *Community and Junior College Journal,* 1974, *44* (9), 14–15.

Baumol, W.J., & Heim, P. On contracting with publishers—or what every author should know. *AAUP Bulletin,* 1967, *53,* 30–46.

Bernstein, T.M. *Miss Thistlebottom's hobgoblins.* New York: Farrar, Straus and Giroux, 1971.

Bloom, H.S., Jr. The teacher's copyright in his teaching materials. *Journal of the Society of Public Teachers of Law,* 1973, *12,* 333–347.

Books in Print. New York: R.R. Bowker, 1948–.

Bowden, N.B., Hutchison, L.E., & Mountain, L. Where to share: A potpourri of reading journals. *The Reading Teacher,* 1977, *30,* 405–411.

Bowden, N.B., & Mountain, L.H. To be or not to be a writer: The how and where of publishing language arts articles. *English Journal,* 1975, *64* (1), 106–109.

Brodbelt, S.S. Research: Unknown, ignored, and misused. *Educational Forum,* 1967, *31,* 151–156.

Brodinsky, B. *Producing better articles for the educational press: A resource.* Glassboro, N.J.: Educational Press Association of America, 1975.

Budahl, L.A. The impending copyright law and the educator. *NASSP Bulletin,* 1971, *55* (357), 41–49.

Burack, A.S. (Ed.) *The writer's handbook.* Boston: The Writer, Inc., 1978.

Cameron, J.R. & Goding, W.E. *A guide to publishing in education: An annotated index.* Calgary, Alberta, Canada: Foothills Educational Press, 1977.

Camp, W.L. *Guide to periodicals in education.* Metuchen, N.J.: Scarecrow Press, 1968.

Camp, W.L., & Schwark, B.L. *Guide to periodicals in education and its academic disciplines.* Metuchen, N.J.: Scarecrow Press, 1975.

Campbell, W.G., & Ballou, S.V. *Form and style: Theses, reports, term papers* (4th ed.). Boston: Ho·ghton Mifflin, 1974.

Caplow, T., & McGee, R.J. *The academic marketplace.* New York: Basic Books, 1958.

Cardozo, M.H. To copy or not to copy for teaching and scholarship: What I tell my client. *Journal of College and University Law,* 1976–77, *4,* 59–81.

Cardozo, M.H. Copyright Act of 1976: A symposium. *UCLA Law Review,* 1977, *24,* 951–1286.

Cassidy, M. *The writer's manual.* Palm Springs, Calif.: ETC Publications, 1979.

Caughran, A.M. The teacher and the copyright law. *Journal of Reading,* 1973, *17,* 8–15.

Centra, J.A. *How universities evaluate faculty performance: A survey of department heads* (GRE Board Research Report GREB No. 75-5bR). Princeton, N.J.: Graduate Record Examination Board, July 1977.

Conklin, F. Writing for publication. *Instructor,* 1968, 77 (10), 96.

Conrad, H.S. Preparation of manuscripts for publication as monographs. *Journal of Psychology,* 1948, *26,* 447–459.

Cox, W.M., & Catt, V. Productivity ratings of graduate programs in psychology based on publications in journals of the American Psychological Association. *American Psychologist,* 1977, *32,* 793–813.

Current contents in social and behavioral sciences. Philadelphia: Institute for Scientific Information, 1978.

Current index to journals in education. Phoenix, Ariz.: Oryx Press, 1979.

Delaney, A.A. Guidelines for the potential teacher-author. *The Clearing House,* 1969, *44,* 210–213.

Dessauer, J.P. *Book publishing: What it is, what it does.* New York: R.R. Bowker Co., 1974.

Directory of publishing opportunities (3rd ed.). Chicago: Marquis Academic Media, 1975.

Education index. New York: H.W. Wilson Co., 1978.

Educational Press Association of America. *America's education press: A classified list of educational periodicals* (33rd ed.). Glassboro, N.J.: Author, 1976.

Educational Researcher, Washington, D.C.: American Educational Research Association, 1978, 7 (5).

Educator's world: The standard guide to American-Canadian educational associations, conventions, foundations, publications and research centers. Philadelphia: North America, 1972.

ERIC processing manual: Rules and guidelines for the acquisition, selection and technical processing of documents and journal articles by the various components of the ERIC network. Washington, D.C.: Educational Resources Information Center, 1974. (ERIC Document Reproduction Service No. ED 092 164).

Etzold, T.H. Writing for publication: The art of the article. *Phi Delta Kappan,* 1976, *57,* 614–615.

Fisk, M. *Encyclopedia of Associations* (12th ed.), Detroit, Mich.: Gale Research Company, 1978.

Frantz, T.T. Criteria for publishable manuscripts. *Personnel and Guidance Journal,* 1968, *47,* 384–386.

Gilbert, M.B. *Clear writing.* New York: John Wiley & Sons, 1977.

Gillespie, J. Personal communication, February 13, 1979.

Gilman, P. Dear contributor: We regret to inform you. *Journal of Teacher Education,* 1978, *29,* 67–68.

Glueck, W.F., & Jauch, L.R. Sources of research ideas among productive scholars: Implications for administrators. *Journal of Higher Education,* 1975, *46,* 103–114.

Hall, D.E., & Blackburn, R.T. *Determinants of faculty publication productivity at four-year colleges.* Paper presented at the annual meeting of the American Educational Research Association, Washington, D.C., April 1975.

Haskell, J.F. Journals, newsletters and other publications for ESL teachers. *TESOL Quarterly,* 1978, *12* (5) , 21–23.

Heilprin, C.B. Technology and the future of the copyright principle. *Phi Delta Kappan,* 1967, *48,* 220–225.

Kaplan, L. Survival talk for educators: Tenure and promotions. *Journal of Teacher Education,* 1977, *28* (5) , 37–38.

Katz, B., & Richards, B. *Magazines for libraries* (4th ed.) . New York: R.R. Bowker, 1978.

Katz, D.A. Faculty salaries, promotions, and productivity at a large university. *American Economic Review,* 1973, *63,* 469–477.

Kimble, G.A. Publication policies of psychological monographs. *American Psychologist,* 1964, *19,* 284–285.

Kingsley, M.S. Evaluating faculty publications. *Liberal Education,* 1976, *62,* 392–400.

Kline, L.W. Editorial: From your pen to the RT page. *The Reading Teacher,* 1972, *26* (1) , 4–6.

Koester, J., & Hillman, G.J. (Eds.) . *1978 writer's market.* Cincinnati, Ohio: Writer's Digest Books, 1977.

Koulack, D., & Kesselman, H.J. Ratings of psychology journals by members of the American Psychological Association. *American Psychologists,* 1975, *30,* 1049–53.

Krepal, W.J., & Duvall, C.K. *Education and education-related serials: A directory.* Littleton, Colo.: Libraries Unlimited, 1977.

Kurlantzick, L. Personal communication, April 28, 1978.

Ladd, E.C., Jr., & Lipset, S.M. What do professors like best about their jobs? Surprise: It isn't research. *The Chronicle of Higher Education,* March 29, 1976, p. 10.

Lewis, L. Publish or perish: Some comments on a hyperbole. *Journal of Higher Education,* 1967, *38,* 85–89.

Library of Congress. *New serial titles: A union list of serials commencing publication after December 31, 1949.* Washington, D.C.: U.S. Government Printing Office, 1977.

Lins, L.J., & Rees, R.A. *Scholars guide to journals of education and educational psychology.* Madison, Wis.: Dembar Educational Research Services, 1965.

Linton, M. *A simplified style manual: For the preparation of jour-*

nal articles in psychology, social sciences, education, and litera-ture. New York: Appleton-Century-Crofts, 1972.

Literary Market Place (1979–1980 ed.). New York: R.R. Bowker, 1979.

Litz, C., & Sparkman, W. What the new copyright law means to educators. *NASSP Bulletin,* 1977, *61* (405), 70–78.

Luce, T.S., & Johnson, D.M. Ratings of educational and psychological journals. *Educational Researcher,* 1978, *7* (10), 8–10.

Macmillan Company. *Guidelines for creating positive sexual and racial images in educational materials.* New York: Author, 1975.

Magarell, J. Copyright law excuses unknowing violators. *The Chronicle of Higher Education,* 1978, *15* (19), 1–10.

Mambert, W.A. *Effective presentation: A short course for professionals.* Washington, D.C.: Capitol Publications, 1976.

McGraw-Hill Book Company. *Guidelines for equal treatment of the sexes in McGraw-Hill Book Company publications.* New York: Author, no date.

Meyer, D. E. To play or not to play—a question. *Educational Forum, 37* (1), 103–104.

Middendorf, G.A. How to submit a manuscript. In *How to get a textbook published.* Symposium presented at the meeting of the American Psychological Association, Division 2, Washington, D.C., September 1976.

Miller, J.K. (Ed.). *Copyright and the teaching/learning process.* Pullman, Wash.: Information Futures, 1977.

Miller, W.C. Writing for journal publication. *Educational Leadership,* 1974, *32,* 51–53.

Modern Language Association of America. *The MLA handbook.* New York: Author, 1977.

Mullins, C.J. *A guide to writing and publishing in the social and behavioral sciences.* New York: John Wiley & Sons, 1977.

Murray, J.F.T. Publish and perish—by suffocation. *Journal of Legal Education,* 1975, *27,* 566–571.

Narin, F., & Garside, D. Journal relationships in special education. *Exceptional Children,* 1972, *38,* 695–703.

National Education Association of the United States. *NEA style manual for writers and editors.* Washington, D.C.: Author, 1966.

National Education Association of the United States. *NEA handbook* (1973–74 ed.) . Washington, D.C.: Author, 1973.

Nelson, C.E. Abstract and information retrieval services in educational research: Current status and planned improvement. *Educational Researcher,* 1974, *3* (10) , 16–18.

The new copyright law and education. Arlington, Va.: Educational Research Service, 1977.

Newman, E. *Strictly speaking: Will America be the death of English?* Indianapolis: Bobbs-Merrill, 1974.

Nimmer, M. *Nimmer on copyright.* New York: Bender, 1972.

Ohles, J.F. Writing for publication. *Clearing House,* 1970, *45,* 245–249.

Palais, E.S. References to indexes and abstracts in Ulrich's International Periodicals Directory, *RQ,* 1974, 34–36.

Penchansky, M. et al. *Publishing: Alternatives and economics.* New York: City University of New York Library Association, 1974. (ERIC Document Reproduction Service No. ED 110 057) .

Pitts, B. E. & Fletcher, R. F. *Southeastern college and university administrators' attitudes toward selected avenues of publication.* Unpublished manuscript, Tennessee Technological University, 1978.

Rainey, B.G. Guidelines: Writing for journals. *Clearing House,* 1973, *48,* 44–49.

Random House. *Guidelines for multi-ethnic/non-sexist survey.* New York: Author, 1975.

Resources in Education. Washington, D.C.: Educational Resources Information Center, 1978.

Ringer, B.R. Finding your way around the new copyright law. *Publishers Weekly,* 1976, *210,* 38–41.

Robinson, P.W., & Higbee, K.L. Publishing a textbook: Advice from authors and publishers. *Teaching of Psychology,* 1978, *5,* 175–181.

Rodriguez, R., & Uhlenberg, D.M. Publish? or perish: The thought. *Journal of Teacher Education,* 1978, *29,* 64–66.

Roesch, W. Teacher as an author: What is the extent of his recognition. *The Clearing House,* 1968, *43,* 73–78.

Schick, G.B. Author and editor: Catechism and strategies. *Journal of Reading,* 1972, *16,* 50–54.

Schlosberg, H. Hints on presenting a paper at an APA convention. *American Psychologist,* 1965, *20,* 606–607.

Scholarly publishing: A journal for author and publisher. Toronto: University of Toronto Press, 1978–.

Sculley, M. Journal costs alarming scholars. *The Chronicle of Higher Education,* November 17, 1975, 8.

Sculley, M. Strained relationships worry scholars: Publishers. *The Chronicle of Higher Education,* January 12, 1976, 1.

Seaton, H.W. Education journals: Publication lags and acceptance rates. *Educational Researcher,* 1975, *4* (4) , 18–19.

Seigfried, J.J., & White, K.J. Teaching and publishing as determinants of academic salaries. *Journal of Economic Education,* 1973, *4,* 90–99.

Showalter, D.E. Publication and stagnation in the liberal arts colleges. *Educational Record,* 1978, *59,* 166–172.

Skillin, M.E., & Gay, R.M. (Eds.) . *Words into type* (3rd ed.) . Englewood Cliffs, N.J.: Prentice-Hall, 1974.

Social sciences citation index. Philadelphia: Institute for Scientific Information, 1978–.

Social sciences index. New York: H.W. Wilson Co., 1978.

Sociology of education abstracts. Elmsford, N.Y.: Maxwell House, 1977.

Spithill, A.C. To leave a scratch on the wall: Getting published. *Personnel and Guidance Journal,* 1973, *52,* 35–38.

Standard periodical directory 1979–1980 (6th ed.) . New York: Oxbridge Communications, 1978.

Strunk, W., Jr., & White, E.B. *The elements of style* (3rd ed.) . New York: Macmillan, 1979.

Silverman, R.J. Diffusion of educational knowledge through journals: Gatekeepers' selection criteria. *Viewpoints in Teaching and Learning,* 1978, *54* (2) , 1–22.

Taubman, J. Copyright and educational media: A symposium. *Performing Arts Review,* 1977, *1,* 1–90. (a)

Taubman, J. Some implications of copyright to the arts and education. *Performing Arts Review,* 1977, *1,* 296–327. (b)

Thesaurus of ERIC descriptors (8th ed.). Phoenix: Oryx Press, summer 1980.

Tuckman, H.P. *Publishing, teaching, and the academic reward structure.* Lexington, Mass.: Lexington Books–D.C. Heath, 1976.

Tuckman, H.P., & Hagmann, R.E. An analysis of the reward structure in two disciplines. *Journal of Higher Education,* 1976, *47,* 447–464.

Turabian, K.L. *A manual for writers of term papers, theses, and dissertations* (3rd ed.). Chicago: University of Chicago Press, 1967.

Turbeville, G. Better to publish than perish. *Education,* 1967, *87,* 416–419.

Uhlan, E. *What every writer should know about publishing his own book.* Hicksville, N.Y.: Exposition Press, 1972.

Uhlan, E. *The rogue of publishers row.* Hicksville, N.Y.: Exposition Press, 1977.

Ulrich's international periodicals directory (18th ed.). New York: R.R. Bowker, 1978.

Ulrich's irregular serials and annuals: An international directory (5th ed.). New York: R.R. Bowker, 1978.

United States Copyright Office. *General guide to the Copyright Act of 1976.* Washington, D.C.: U.S. Government Printing Office, 1977.

United States Copyright Office. *Circular R 21: Reproduction of copyrighted works by educators and librarians.* Washington, D.C.: U.S. Government Printing Office, 1978.

United States Government Printing Office. *Style manual* (rev. ed.). Washington, D.C.: Author, 1973.

United States House of Representatives. *Report No. 94–1476,* 94th Congress, 2nd Session, 1976.

University of Chicago Press. *A manual of style* (11th ed.). Chicago: Author, 1949.

University of Chicago Press. *A manual of style* (12th ed.). Chicago: Author, 1969.

University Press of America. *A timely approach to publishing from University Press of America.* Washington, D.C.: Author, no date.

U.S. News and World Report, Inc. *U.S. News and World Report stylebook for writers and editors.* Washington, D.C.: Author, 1977.

van Leunen, M.C. *A handbook for scholars.* New York: Alfred A. Knopf, 1978. (a)

van Leunen, M.C. Scholarship: A singular notion. *The Atlantic,* 1978, *241* (5) , 88–89. (b)

Van Til, W. Writing for educational publication. *Phi Delta Kappan,* 1973, *54,* 700–701.

Van Til, W. Editorial roulette. *Phi Delta Kappan,* 1978, *59,* 417–418.

Van Til, W. *Writing for educational publication.* Bloomington: Indiana State University Closed Circuit Television Center, no date. (Video tape)

Walberg, H.J. University distinction in educational research: An exploratory survey. *Educational Researcher,* 1972, *1* (1) , 15–16.

Wall, J. Getting into print in P & G: How it's done. *Personnel and Guidance Journal,* 1974, *52,* 594–602.

Ward, H.W., Hall, B.W., & Schramm, C.F. Evaluation of published educational research: A national survey. *American Educational Research Journal,* 1975, *12,* 109–128.

Wentling, T.L. *Publish or perish.* Workshop presented at the meeting of the American Vocational Association, Atlantic City, N.J., December 4, 1977.

West, C.K. Productivity ratings of institutions based on publications in the journals of the American Education Research Association: 1970–1976. *Educational Researcher,* 1978, 7 (2) , 13–14.

Wigren, H.E. Don't touch! This is copyrighted. *Educational Leadership,* 1968, *26,* 254–257.

Wilson, L. *The academic man: A study in the sociology of a profession.* New York: Oxford University Press, 1942.

Yorkey, R. How to prepare and present a professional paper. *TESOL newsletter,* 1978, *12* (1) , 3–4.

Zeiger, H.P. Suggestions to authors from a reviewer. In *How to get a textbook published.* Symposium presented at the meeting of the American Psychological Association, Division 2, Washington, D.C., September 1976.

Zirkel, P.A. Copyright law in higher education: Individuals, institutions, and innovations. *Journal of College and University Law*, 1976, *2*, 342–353.

Zirkel, P.A. Writing for educational publications. *Journal of Teacher Education*, 1978, *29*, 69.

Zurcher, L.A., Jr. The many faces of Don Quixote—at a social science convention, *Journal of Applied Behavioral Science*, 1977, *13*, 225–236.

Index